Sepoys, Siege & Storm

Sepoys, Siege & Storm

The Experiences of a Young Officer
of H. M. 61st Regt. at Ferozepore,
on Delhi Ridge and at the
Fall of Delhi During
the Indian Mutiny

Charles John Griffiths
Late Captain 61st Regiment

Edited by Henry John Yonge
Late Captain 61st Regiment

LEONAUR

Sepoys, Siege & Storm: The Experiences of a Young Officer of H. M. 61st Regt. at Ferozepore, on Delhi Ridge and at the Fall of Delhi During the Indian Mutiny
by Charles John Griffiths

Originally published under the title:
A Narrative of The Siege of Delhi
With an Account of the Mutiny At Ferozepore In 1857

Published by Leonaur Ltd

ISBN (10 digit): 1-84677-097-1 (hardcover)
ISBN (13 digit): 978-1-84677-097-5 (hardcover)

ISBN (10 digit): 1-84677-089-0 (softcover)
ISBN (13 digit): 978-1-84677-089-0 (softcover)

http://www.leonaur.com

Publisher's Notes

In the interests of authenticity, the spellings, grammar and place names used have been retained from the original editions.

The opinions of the authors represent a view of events in which he was a participant related from his own perspective, as such the text is relevant as an historical document.

The views expressed in this book are not necessarily those of the publisher.

Contents

Introduction

The ever memorable period in the history of our Eastern Empire known as the Great Indian Rebellion or Mutiny of the Bengal army was an epoch fraught with the most momentous consequences, and one which resulted in covering with undying fame those who bore part in its suppression. The passions aroused during the struggle, the fierce hate animating the breasts of the combatants, the deadly incidents of the strife, which without intermission lasted for nearly two years, and deluged with blood the plains and cities of Hindostan, have scarcely a parallel in history. On the one side religious fanaticism, when Hindoo and Mohammedan, restraining the bitter animosity of their rival creeds, united together in the attempt to drive out of their common country that race which for one hundred years had dominated and held the overlordship of the greater portion of India. On the other side, a small band of Englishmen, a few thousand white men among millions of Asiatics, stood shoulder to shoulder, calm, fearless, determined, ready to brave the onslaught of their enemies, to maintain with undiminished lustre the proud deeds of their ancestors, and to a man resolved to conquer or to die.

Who can recount the numberless acts of heroism, the hairbreadth escapes, the anxious days and nights passed by our gallant countrymen, who, few in number, and isolated from their comrades, stood at bay in different parts of the land surrounded by hundreds of pitiless miscreants, tigers in human shape thirsting for their blood? And can pen describe the nameless horrors of the time—gently nurtured ladies outraged and slain before the eyes of their husbands, children and helpless infants slaughtered—a very Golgotha of butchery, as all know who have read of the Well of Cawnpore?

The first months of the rebellion were a fight for dear life, a constant struggle to avert entire annihilation, for to all who were there it seemed as though no power on earth could save them. But Providence willed it otherwise, and after the full extent of the danger was realized, gloomy forebodings gave way to stern endeavours. Men arose, great in council and in the field, statesmen and warriors—Lawrence, Montgomery, Nicholson, Hodson, and many others. The crisis brought to the front numbers of daring spirits, full of energy and resource, of indomitable resolution and courage, men who from the beginning saw the magnitude of the task set before them, and with calm judgment faced the inevitable. These were they who saved our Indian Empire, and who, by the direction of their great organized armies, brought those who but a few years before had been our mortal enemies to fight cheerfully on our side, and, carrying to a successful termination the leaguer of Delhi, stemmed the tide of the rebellion, and broke the backbone of the Mutiny.

The interest excited amongst all classes of our countrymen by the events which happened during the momentous crisis of 1857 in India can scarcely be appreciated by the present generation. So many years have elapsed that all those who held high commands or directed the councils of the Government have long since died, and the young participants in the contest who survived its toils and dangers are all now past middle age. But the oft-told tale will still bear repetition, and the recital of the achievements of Englishmen during the great Indian rebellion will fill the hearts of their descendants for all time with pride, and incite them to emulate their actions. In the hour of danger the heart of the nation is stirred to its profoundest depths, the national honour is at stake, and that heritage bequeathed to us by our ancestors must at all hazards be preserved. Thus it happened in 1857, and the result is well known. So it may again occur, and with confidence it may be predicted that, as of yore, Britain's sons will not be found wanting in the hour of trial, that, keeping well in mind the glorious traditions of their race, they will maintain unsullied the reputation of their forefathers, and add to the renown of that Empire on which the sun never sets.

It is unnecessary, in this place, to enter into the causes which led to the mutiny of the Bengal army. These can be read and studied in the graphic pages of Kaye and Malleson. My intention is to give, as far as in me lies, a truthful account of the events in which I personally bore part, and which came under my own immediate observation.

CHAPTER 1
Ferozepore

The actual Mutiny of the Bengal army broke out at Meerut on May 10, 1857. Events had happened in the Lower Provinces which foreshadowed the coming storm, and one regiment of native infantry had been disbanded; but no one, not even those in high authority, had the faintest suspicion that our rule in India was imperilled. So strong, indeed, was the sense of security from present danger that the Government, with almost culpable neglect, still confided to the care of the native army the large arsenals of Delhi, Ferozepore, and Phillour, in all of which immense quantities of ammunition and munitions of war were stored.

There was not a single white regiment stationed at Delhi, not even a European guard, the charge of the arsenal, the largest in Upper India, being entrusted to a few officers and sergeants of artillery. The same may be said of Phillour, in the Punjab—a small station, where only native troops were quartered. The fort of Ferozepore, near the left bank of the Sutlej River, was guarded by 100 men detailed from the sepoy regiments at that cantonment, and, with Phillour, constituted the only places from which ammunition could be drawn for the large force, European and native, guarding the newly-acquired province of the Punjab.

Her Majesty's 61st Regiment of Foot was stationed at Ferozepore in May, 1857. In that corps I held a commission as Lieutenant, and, during the absence of my Captain on leave in Kashmir, was in temporary command of the Grenadier Company.

The regiment at this time mustered nearly 1,000 men, half that number old and gallant veterans of from ten to twenty years' service. These had fought in many Indian campaigns, and on the terrible day of Chillianwalla, in January, 1849, when the Khalsa army rolled back in utter defeat a portion of Lord Gough's force, had, under the leadership of Sir Colin Campbell, altered the fortunes of the battle. Advancing in line under a tremendous cannonade, and without firing a shot, they marched as if on parade and in stern silence till within fifty yards of the Sikh batteries, when, with a shout which struck terror into the breasts of their enemies, they charged irresistibly and took the guns.

It was to men such as these that, fortunately for the maintenance of our Empire in the East, England trusted in the perilous days of 1857. As of my own regiment, so it may be said of all then quartered in India—sturdy, fine fellows, of good physique, of rare discipline, and inured to the climate, who, in the words of the Iron Duke, could march anywhere and fight anything. The army then had not been improved out of existence; reforms, if such they can be called, were received with considerable disfavour; for what amelioration could be effected in the discipline and steady courage of those who had stormed the heights of the Alma, had stood the shock of the Muscovite at Inkerman, and had not despaired on the bloody fields of Ferozeshah and Chillianwalla?

I may be excused if I thus energetically offer my tribute of praise to that army, and more especially to that regiment in which I passed my young days. I recall the numberless acts of devotion and courage, the tender solicitude with which the veterans of the Grenadier Company looked after the safety of their youthful commander, during the campaigns of 1857; and my pen falters and my eyes grow dim with tears as memory brings before me my gallant comrades in the ranks who fell before Delhi, or lost their lives through disease and exposure.

I had been absent from my regiment during the whole of 1856, doing duty at the Murree Convalescent Depot, and rejoined in March of the following year. Nothing occurred for the next two months to break the monotony of life in an Indian cantonment. Parade in the early morning, rackets and billiards during the day, a drive or ride along the Mall in the cool of the evening, and the usual mess dinner—these constituted the routine of our uneventful existence.

Many of the officers lamented the hard fate which had doomed them to service in the East, while the more fortunate regiments had been earning fame and quick promotion in the Crimea and in the recent Persian campaign. We little thought of what was in store for us, or of the volcano which was smouldering under our feet.

The signs of incipient mutiny in the native army had been confined, up to this time, to the Presidency of Bengal and to the regiments quartered there. With us at Ferozepore there was little, if any, indication of the coming outbreak. True it was that some of us noticed sullen looks and strange demeanour among the sepoys of the two battalions. They, on occasions, passed our officers without the customary salute, and, if my memory serves, a complaint of this want of respect was forwarded to their Colonels. Our billiard-marker, too, a high-caste Brahmin who had served on our side in the Afghan campaigns of 1839-42 in the capacity of a spy, a man of cunning and intelligence, warned us in unmistakable terms of the increasing disaffection among the sepoys of Ferozepore, and stated his opinion that the spirit of mutiny was rife among them. We laughed at his fears, and dismissed from our minds all alarm, vaunting our superiority in arms to the dusky soldiery of Hindostan, and in our hearts foolishly regarding them with lordly contempt.

Thus passed in the usual quiet the first twelve days of the month of May, 1857. The morning of May 13 saw us, as usual, on parade; then, adjourning to the mess-house, we spent a few hours over breakfast and billiards, and before midday separated to pass the heat of the day reading, lounging, and sleeping at our respective bungalows.

I occupied a large house some distance from the mess in company with a field-officer and the Adjutant of my regiment. The former, about 1 p. m., was summoned by an orderly to attend a meeting at the quarters of the Brigadier[1] commanding the troops at Ferozepore. We paid no heed to this incident, as it occurred to us that the Major's advice and opinion were required on some matter of regimental or other routine.

Vicars and I were in the habit, since the hot weather began, of making ices every afternoon, and had become, from long practice, quite proficient at the work. At three o'clock we were in the midst of our occupation, our whole thoughts and energies bent on the accomplishment of our task. Clad in loose *déshabillé*, seated on the floor of the sitting-room, we worked and watched the process of congelation.

Presently a quick step was heard in the hall, the door was thrown open, and the Major, rushing in, sank breathless into a chair. The Adjutant and I jumped up, and in our haste upset the utensils, spilling on the floor the contents we had taken so much trouble to prepare. A minute or two passed, and still no word from our friend, who, portly in shape, and of a plethoric temperament, seemed overcome by some terrible excitement, and fairly gasped for breath.

"What on earth is the matter?" we asked.

Slowly, and as though uttered with considerable difficulty, the answer came:

"All the Europeans in India have been murdered!"

1: Brigadier-General Innes

Now this was rather a startling announcement, and somewhat premature, considering that we three, at any rate, were in the land of the living, with no immediate prospect of coming dissolution. We looked at each other, at first serious and alarmed, as became the gravity of the situation, and utterly unable to comprehend what it all meant. This phase of the affair, however, did not last long, and soon changed from grave to gay. A merry twinkle appeared in Vicars' eyes, to which my own responded, and at last, fully alive to the absurdity of the gallant officer's remark, our pent-up sense of the ridiculous was fairly awakened, and we roared with laughter again and again.

This unlooked-for result of his dismal communication roused the Major, who first rebuked us for our levity, and, after an interval occupied in the recovery of his scattered senses, proceeded to acquaint us with the true facts of what had happened at the Brigadier's quarters.

A despatch by telegraph had arrived that morning from Meerut, the largest cantonment in Upper India, stating that the regiment of Native Light Cavalry at that place had mutinied in a body on the 10th instant, and marched for Delhi. This had been followed by a revolt of all the sepoy infantry and artillery, a rising of the natives in the city, the bazaars and the surrounding country, who, almost unchecked, had murdered the European men and women on whom they could lay their hands, and besides, had set fire to and "looted" many houses in the station. Fortunately for the safety of the English in India, the miscreants failed to cut the telegraph-wires at Meerut till too late, and the news of the mutiny and outrage was as quickly as possible flashed to every cantonment in the country.

The Brigadier had therefore ordered the commanding and field officers of the different regiments stationed at Ferozepore to meet him in consultation at his quarters. Intelligence so startling as that just received required no small amount of judgment and deliberation in dealing with the native soldiers at this cantonment, and some time elapsed before the council decided as to what was best to be done under the circumstances.

Finally it was resolved that a general parade of Her Majesty's 61st Foot and the battery of European artillery should be held at four o'clock on the lines in front of the barracks of the former corps. The two regiments of native infantry were to assemble at the same time, and, with their English Officers, were ordered to march from their quarters, taking separate directions: the 45th to proceed into the country, leaving the fort of Ferozepore on their right, while the 57th were to march out of cantonments to the left rear of the lines of the European infantry. The commanding officers of these regiments were also instructed to keep their men, if possible, well in hand, to allow no straggling, and to halt in the country until further orders after they had proceeded three or four miles. The remaining regiment, the 10th Native Light Cavalry, for some reason or other was considered staunch (and as events proved, it remained so for a time), and it was therefore ordained that the troopers should parade mounted and under arms in their own lines ready for any emergency.

Thus far we learnt from the Major, and Vicars, whose duties as Adjutant required his presence at the barracks at once, donned his uniform, and, mounting his horse, rode in all haste to give directions for the general parade.

Shortly before four o'clock the Major and I also left the house and joined the regiment, which was drawn up in open column of companies in front of the lines.

Notice had previously been sent to the married officers in the station directing them to make immediate arrangements for the transport of their wives and families to the barracks. This order was obeyed without loss of time, and before half-past four all the ladies and children in the cantonment were safe under the protection of our soldiers at the main guard.

The barracks of the European infantry at Ferozepore were distant half a mile from the station, and consisted of ten or twelve large detached buildings, one for each company, arranged in echelon, with some thirty paces between each. In front of these was the parade-ground where we were drawn up, and before us an open plain, 300 yards in width, extending to the entrenched camp, or, as it was generally called, the fort and arsenal of Ferozepore. The space around the fort was quite clear, its position being directly opposite the centre of the cantonment, from which it was separated by some 200 yards.

From our situation on parade we had a direct and unbroken view of the localities I have endeavoured to describe, and holding this vantage-ground, we should be enabled to act as circumstances might require.

The regiment wheeled into line more than 900 strong. One hundred men under command of a field-officer were then detached, with orders to disarm the sepoy guard in the fort, and to remain there on duty pending any attempt which might probably be made by the two native regiments to gain forcible possession of the arsenal.

The detachment marched off, and we watched our comrades cross the plain, and enter without molestation the gates of the fort.

In anxious expectation we waited for the result, when, after a short interval, shots were heard, and we knew that our men had engaged the sepoy guard. The firing was continuous while it lasted, but soon died away. A mounted officer then rode out at the gate, and, galloping to where the Colonel was standing, reported that the sepoys, when ordered to lay down their arms, refused, and that one of them, taking direct aim at the Major,[2] shot him in the thigh, leaving a dangerous wound. Our men then poured a volley into

---

2: Major Redmond

17

the mutineers, who fired in return, but fortunately without causing any casualty on our side. Two sepoys had been killed and several wounded, while the remainder, offering no further resistance, were disarmed and made prisoners.

Meantime the regiment stood under arms in line, and another company was sent to reinforce the men in the fort.

Amid great excitement, more especially among the young soldiers, we waited to see what would follow when the sepoy battalions marching from cantonments into the country appeared in sight. Eagerly it was whispered amongst us, "Will the rascals fight, or remain loyal and obedient to the orders of their officers?"

The evening was drawing on apace, but at last, about six o'clock, the heads of the columns emerged from the houses and gardens of the station, the 45th Native Infantry advancing in almost a direct line to the fort, while the 57th Native Infantry were inclined to their right, and followed the road leading to the rear of our lines. All eyes were turned on the former regiment, and its movements were ardently scanned.

Closer and closer they came to the fort, till, when only about fifty paces distant, the column wavered. We could see the officers rushing about among their men, and in another instant the whole mass broke into disorder and ran pell-mell in hundreds towards the ditch which surrounded the entrenchment.

This was of no depth, with sloping sides, and easy to escalade, and in less time than I take to write it the sepoys, with a shout, jumped into the trench, scrambled up the parapet, and disappeared from our sight into the enclosure.

It was not long before we heard the sound of firing, and shots came in quick succession, maddening us beyond control, for we thought of our men, few in number and scattered over the fort, opposed to some five or six hundred of these savages.

We had loaded with ball-cartridge soon after forming on parade, and the men now grasped their muskets, and cries and murmurs were heard, "Why do we not advance?" and all this couched in language more forcible than polite.

The order at last was given to fix bayonets, and then came the welcome words:

"The line will advance."

Every heart thrilled with excitement. All longed to have a brush with the mutineers, and help our comrades in the fort who were fighting against such odds.

Twenty paces only we advanced, and then, by the Brigadier's command, our Colonel[3] gave the order to halt.

The men were furious, and could hardly be restrained from marching forward, when, looking towards the outer side of the fort, we saw some sepoys on the ramparts, evidently in a state of panic, throw themselves into the ditch, and mounting the other side, run helterhelterskelter into the country. These were followed by numbers of others, who all made off as fast as their legs would carry them, and then we heard a true British cheer, our men appeared on the walls shooting at the fugitives, bayonetting and driving them over the glacis.

The fight had continued some twenty minutes, and was pretty severe while it lasted. A few of our men were more or less hurt, but of the sepoys many had been killed and wounded. About 100 also had laid down their arms, and, begging for mercy, were taken prisoners.

Nothing could have been more culpable than the conduct of the Brigadier in not advancing a portion, at any rate, of my regiment to the fort at the time the sepoys broke their ranks and entered the entrenchment. Had he done so, it is probable that not one of the mutineers of the 45th Native Infantry would have escaped, nor would the havoc which afterwards

---

3: Colonel William Jones, C.B.

occurred in the cantonment have taken place. But he was an old East India Company's officer, and had served upwards of forty years in the native army, having to the last, like many others at that eventful time, implicit confidence in the loyalty of the sepoys. He feared, also, the responsibility of letting loose the English soldiery to wreak their vengeance on the mutineers, knowing too well that, with passions roused and hearts steeled to pity by the murders and outrages committed at Meerut, and the late wounding of their field-officer, our men would have given no quarter. The Brigadier was one of the very few officers in high command at the outbreak of the Mutiny who were found wanting in the time of trial. His, no doubt, was a hard task; but, had he shown the smallest aptitude to meet the crisis, there would have been no difficulty, with the ample means at his disposal, in disarming without bloodshed the whole native force at Ferozepore, and so crushing the rebellion at that station.

Night came, and we still remained in line under arms without having moved a foot from where we were halted. Conjectures were rife as to what would next happen. Officers and men were grieved, no less than annoyed, at the state of inaction in which we had been kept, and an uneasy feeling prevailed that during the night the mutinous sepoys, aided by the *badmashes*, or bad characters, who swarmed in the bazaars and city of Ferozepore, would, under cover of the darkness, run riot over the cantonment, without our being called on to interfere.

And so, unhappily, it came to pass. The native cavalry at about eight o'clock marched down to our lines, and drew up on the right of the regiment, the European artillery being on our left flank.

Soon after their arrival the arms were piled and the men fell out of the ranks, some to lie down on the ground, others forming in groups and discussing the strange events of the day.

20

Suddenly a light was seen in the direction of the cantonment, which quickly turned into a blaze of fire. What new horror was this? Were our houses to be gutted and burnt before our eyes without any attempt to prevent such outrage?

The men, at the first appearance of fire, had sprung to their feet and almost involuntarily seized their arms. Surely a detachment would be sent to clear the cantonment of the incendiaries? Even this was not done: the Brigadier was absent, or could not be found, and our Colonel intimated to some officers who spoke to him on the subject that he could give no orders without the chief's consent.

So, incredible though it may appear, we stood and watched the fires, which followed each other in quick succession till the whole cantonment seemed in a blaze, and the flames, darting up in every direction, lighted up the surrounding country.

We could hear distinctly the shouts of the scoundrels, and pictured to ourselves the black wretches holding high carnival among the burning buildings and laughing at the white soldiers, who, with arms in their hands, remained motionless in their own lines.

That night more than twenty houses were burnt to the ground. The English church, we afterwards heard, was first fired, then the Roman Catholic chapel, our mess-house, and nineteen other bungalows. The sepoys, mostly of the 45th Native Infantry, attended by dozens of *badmashes*, marched unchallenged through the station with lighted torches fixed on long bamboo poles, with which they set fire to the thatched roofs of the various houses.

All night long we lay by our arms, watching the destruction of our property, and thankful only that the wives and children of our officers and men were safe under our care, and not exposed to the fury of the wretches engaged in their fiendish work.

Even after this long lapse of years, I cannot think of that night without a feeling of shame. Here were 700 men, mostly veterans, of one of Her Majesty's regiments, doomed to inaction through the blundering and stupid perverseness of an old sepoy Brigadier. The same unhappy events as those I have narrated occurred at the outbreak of the Mutiny in three other stations in the Bengal Presidency.

The commanders would not act against their trusted sepoys, who, as in our case, plundered, outraged, and destroyed all and everything that came in their way.

May 14.—The morning of May 14 dawned, close and hot, not a breath of wind stirring. The sun rose like a ball of fire, and shortly afterwards we were startled by an explosion which shook the earth under our feet, and sounded like a heavy peal of thunder in the still morning air. Looking in the direction of the report, we saw on the far right side of the cantonment a thick black column of smoke shoot up high into the atmosphere. A quarter of an hour passed, and then another detonation similar to the first sounded in our ears on the left rear flank, followed, as before, by a dense cloud of smoke.

We said to ourselves: "Will the arsenal next be blown up?" In the fort was stored an immense quantity of powder and munitions of war, and, fearing that perhaps some rebel might have found his way in for the purpose of devoting his life to the destruction of the entrenchment and the annihilation of the European guard, we remained anxiously expectant for some time.

No cause could be assigned for the explosions we had heard, but we were informed subsequently that, by the orders of our commander, the magazines or bells of arms belonging to the two native regiments had been blown up by a party of sappers in the fear that they might fall into the hands of the rebellious sepoys. It was a futile precaution, and a mere waste of ammunition; for nothing could have been easier than to send the contents of the magazines under our escort to the arsenal.

At eight o'clock we were dismissed to barracks, and left the spot where we had stood in line inert and inactive since four o'clock the previous afternoon.

Shortly after breakfast I was sent for by the Colonel to the orderly-room, and informed that it was the wish of the Brigadier that I should proceed with my company into the cantonments. I was ordered to make strict search for, and to take prisoner, any sepoys or bad characters that might be lurking about; and to this end I was to patrol the station from one side to the other. I was also to visit the commissariat quarters, disarm the native guard, using force if necessary, and secure the treasure chest, which contained some 20,000 rupees.

It struck me that this duty might very well have been performed many hours before. Why had not a company been detailed to patrol the cantonment the previous evening, or, at any rate, at the first sign of incendiarism?

However, I started without delay with ninety Grenadiers, and marched over a great part of the station, extending the company in skirmishing order whenever we passed through the numerous large gardens, orchards, and enclosures.

Not a soul was to be seen, and the place seemed entirely deserted. The sepoys, after their work of destruction, must have left during the night, and were now probably well on their way to Delhi, while the *badmashes* who had assisted them had returned quietly to their occupations in the bazaars of the city.

The cantonment presented a complete scene of desolation. The church and chapel were a heap of burnt-up and smouldering ruins, our mess-house the same, and numerous bungalows—former residences of the officers—were still on fire. The heat from the burning embers was intense, and as we passed slowly by we viewed, with anger in our hearts, the lamentable results of the timidity and vacillation, the irresolution and culpable neglect, of one man.

Lastly, we visited the commissariat quarters at the far side of the station. Here there was no guard, not even a native in charge. Strange inconsistency! It turned out that, some hours before our arrival, the sepoy guard, true in this respect to their trust, had procured a cart, taken the treasure to the fort, there handed it over to the officer at the gate, and then started for Delhi.

My duty was accomplished, and I marched the Grenadiers back to barracks, then reported the unsatisfactory result of my mission to the Colonel; and, thoroughly tired and worn out from want of rest, I threw myself on a bed and slept soundly for some hours.

We were told that afternoon that the 57th Native Infantry, who had marched to the rear of our barracks the evening before, had remained quietly in the country during the night without one sepoy showing any mutinous disposition. In the early morning, without molesting their English officers, about half the regiment signified their intention of marching down-country; while of the rest, some 300 men returned to their lines at Ferozepore, and on being called upon to do so by the Colonel, laid down their arms.

It must be recorded to the credit of these regiments that no officer was hurt by them, or even insulted. The sepoys quietly but firmly announced that they released themselves from the service of the East India Company, and were about to become enrolled as subjects of the King of Delhi. Then, in several instances even saluting their officers and showing them every mark of respect, they turned their faces to the great focus of rebellion, to swell the number of those who were about to fight against us in the Mohammedan capital of Hindostan.

The officers of these two corps were more fortunate than their comrades of other regiments throughout the land, many of whom were shot down by their own sepoys in cold blood under circumstances of signal barbarity. They saw their wives and children murdered before their faces, while those who escaped the fury of the sepoys wandered in helpless flight through jungles and plains, suffering incredible privations. Some few there were who reached a friendly station, or were succoured and hidden by loyal natives. But the greater number fell by the hands of the wretches who in these times of outrage and anarchy swarmed out of the low quarters of the cities, and swept unchecked over the whole country in hundreds and thousands.

The officers had taken up their quarters in the barracks in one or the centre buildings, which was reserved entirely for their use. Here we endeavoured to make ourselves as comfortable as possible under the circumstances, the large apartment serving at once as mess-house sitting-room and bedroom for us all. The Colonel alone lived apart, while the married ladies and their families for the present occupied the main guard bungalow pending arrangements for more suitable quarters.

The poor ladies, as was natural, were in a state of great agitation, and would not be comforted. We did our best to quiet their fears, telling them there was not the slightest danger as regarded their safety; that, even were we attacked by the rebels, they need have no dread of the result, for we were more than a match for double our number of sepoys. Still, it pained us much to see their distress, and we could only be thankful that, come what might, they were under the protection of British soldiers.

On the evening of May 14, at sunset, I was sitting smoking and chatting in the barrack-room with some of our officers when, quite unexpectedly, I was again called to the orderly-room, and directed to march with the Grenadier company on outlying picket to the left rear of the cantonment, and close to the lines of the disarmed sepoys. Two guns of the Light Field Battery, under a subaltern, were also placed under my orders, and I took with me a young ensign to assist me in my duties.

The Brigadier said he had received intelligence that an attack by the mutineers was expected from the direction of Lahore; and I was told to keep a sharp lookout, in case the enemy made during the night a flank movement on the station. I was also constantly to patrol the lines of the native regiments, to confine the sepoys to their huts, and to take prisoner any who ventured outside.

The short Indian twilight was drawing to a close when I arrived on the ground, and, without losing time, I drew up the Grenadiers in line, with the two guns a little in advance and on my left flank.

Two sentries were posted in front of the guns, two on the right and left of my small detachment, and two in the rear.

The plain extended before us for miles to the horizon, bare and treeless, without one intervening obstacle.

Evening closed and night came on—a night dark as Erebus, though the stars shone bright and luminous in the heavens. All nature was silent as the grave, and, save for the tramp of the sentinels and the marching away and return of the patrolling parties, for hours we heard no sound.

Before leaving barracks the picket had loaded the guns with grape and the old Brown Bess (there were no rifles in most of the Indian regiments in those far-off days) with ball-cartridge. I had also ordered the men to fix bayonets, and we were thus fully prepared to give a warm reception to any sepoys who might attack us. The arms were piled, and in silence we lay on the ground.

Presently, about midnight, one of the sentinels in front of the guns challenged:

"Who comes there?"

26

There was no answer, and the cry was repeated, the sentry at the same moment firing off his musket.

The company sprang to their arms, and I called on the sentries in front to retreat under cover of the guns. Almost simultaneously, and before the men could retire, flashes of fire appeared on the plain, and numerous shots came whistling over our heads, while, clear and distinct, a cry rang out, and we knew that one of the sentries had been hit. Close following the first came several straggling shots, but the rascals fired too high, and we had no casualty. I then ordered the men to fire a volley, and the artillery officer at the same time swept his front with grape from the two guns.

After these discharges all was still, and we strained our eyes in the darkness, but could see nothing. Then, taking with me a sergeant and four men, I proceeded to where the sentry had made the first challenge.

We found the poor fellow lying face downwards on the ground, and raising him up, saw that he was quite dead. Slowly and tenderly the body was borne to the picket, and on examination by the light of a lantern, we discovered that he had received a bullet over the region of the heart, and that death, therefore, must have been instantaneous. My heart sickened at the sight; this was my first contact with the horrors of war, and the remembrance will remain with me to my dying day.

The other sentinel was then questioned, and from him we learnt that, peering through the darkness when the challenge was first given, he had seen figures passing in his front across the plain. Soon they halted and fired, and then disappeared, probably having lain down to escape being hit by our men. Hearing this, I sent out a small reconnoitring party, which patrolled the plain for some distance. They returned with the news that all was quiet, and no human being was to be seen. Two fresh sentries were placed in front of the guns, and the men lay down as before, fully expecting another attack.

May 15.—All, however, passed off without further incident, and at sunrise I marched the picket to barracks and reported myself to the Brigadier. He made no comment on the events of the night, nor did he even ask for particulars as to the manner of the soldier's death. The mutineers, he said, were in scattered detachments still, no doubt prowling about the outskirts of the cantonment and in the neighbouring villages, taking advantage of every opportunity to harass and inflict loss on our soldiers.

From this time forward for nearly a month, with the single exception of one encounter with a body of mutineers, which I shall relate hereafter, no event of importance occurred at Ferozepore.

The chief danger had passed from our midst in the flight towards Delhi of more than half of the two battalions of sepoys, the disarmament of 300 of the 57th, and the imprisonment of those who had been captured fighting when attempting to take the arsenal.

Everything being thus comparatively peaceful, with no enemy in the vicinity, the Brigadier at last woke up to a sense of his duty; and extraordinary measures were taken by his command for the safety of the cantonments and lines of Ferozepore.

It was ordered that one company should be placed each night on advanced outlying picket, another on rear picket, and a third to be stationed at the main guard to furnish sentries as a cordon round the whole extent of the barracks. Two companies were to remain constantly in the fort in charge of a senior Captain, so that, out of the ten companies, six were always on duty.

Under the excitement which first prevailed, and the necessity of being prepared in case of a night attack from the roving bands of rebellious soldiery who from all directions were making for the imperial city, plundering and ravaging on the route, this duty was cheerfully undertaken. But as time went by, and week succeeded week, without a shot being fired to relieve the monotony of our lives, the work became irksome in the extreme.

The regiment therefore fell into a regular groove of guard and picket duty. We longed to have a fight with the enemy, and still were doomed to remain in a state of masterly inactivity. At the fort the work was most trying, and resolved itself into a course of manual labour. There it was ordered that under the ammunition sheds deep pits were to be dug in the ground. This duty was performed entirely by the English soldiers, and continued for a fortnight in the hottest season of the year. In the receptacles thus formed all the barrels of powder, as well as the small arms, ammunition, etc., were packed and stowed away, the whole being covered with earth to the depth of several feet. This was a very needful expedient, for a stray spark might have blown up the vast stores of munitions of war, without which it would have been impossible to carry on future operations against the enemy. No fires for any purpose were permitted in the fort, and, greatest deprivation of all, the men were not allowed to smoke during the twenty-four hours they were on guard.

Three or four days after the outbreak, and when everything seemed quiet in and around the cantonment, two officers and myself, taking with us some native labourers carrying spades and shovels, proceeded, under orders from our Colonel, to search for the silver plate buried under the ruins of our mess-house. We found the brick walls standing; but all inside the building was one mass of ashes and still-smouldering embers.

We knew the locality of the plate chest, and, setting the coolies to work, after infinite labour, which lasted some hours, we succeeded in removing a vast heap of cinders, and found portions of the silver. A little lower down we came on more; and here were seen spoons melted almost out of shape by fire. The large silver dishes, plates and cups—many of the latter of priceless value, for they had been acquired by the regiment during the Peninsular War—were lying one on top of the other just as they had been placed in the chest, but all ruined and disfigured, half melted and blackened from the intense heat.

Close by, where they had fallen off a table, were the four massive silver candelabra, the gift of distinguished officers who had formerly served in the corps. These were twisted out of all shape, and beyond hope of repair, of no value but for the bullion. Other articles there were, such as snuff-boxes, drinking-horns, and table ornaments; not one single piece of silver had escaped the action of the fire.

It was a sorry sight to look on the total destruction of our beautiful mess furniture. Costly goods had been sacrificed which no money could replace; not one single article belonging to the officers had been saved.

Gathering together all the silver we could find, and lamenting the incompetence by which we had lost property amounting in value to £2,000, we placed everything in a cart and conveyed it to the barracks.

Many months afterwards the Government directed a committee of officers to value the effects destroyed by the mutineers, to the end that remuneration might be granted to the regiment for loss sustained. This committee, after due consideration, placed the estimate at a very low figure—viz., £1,500. The parsimony of those in power refused us full payment of this just debt, intimated also that the demand was exorbitant, and closed all further action in the matter by sending us a draft on the Treasury for half the amount claimed.

For the first week or ten days after the outbreak at Ferozepore we knew very little of what was occurring down-country, as well as throughout the Punjab, the province of the "Five Rivers" to our north. In that newly-acquired territory there were twenty-six regiments of the native army, while the Sikhs, the warlike people who inhabited the land, had met us in deadly conflict only nine years before. From the latter, then, as well as from the sepoys, there was cause for great anxiety. Every precaution, therefore, was necessary to guard the Ferozepore Arsenal, the largest, next to Delhi, in Upper India. The temper of the Sikhs was uncertain; no one could foretell which side they would take in the coming struggle. Our Empire in Hindostan—during the month of May more especially—trembled in the balance. There was infinite cause for alarm for months afterwards even to the Fall of Delhi; but at no time were we in such a strait as at that period when the loyalty or defection of the Sikh regiments and people was an open question.

The genius of Sir John Lawrence, the Chief Commissioner of the Punjab, warded off the danger. That eminent man, the saviour of India, issued a proclamation calling on the Sikhs to aid us in our trouble. They came at once in hundreds—nay, thousands—to enlist on our side. Veterans of Runjeet Singh's Khalsa army, the men who had withstood us on equal terms in many sanguinary battles, animated by intense hatred of the Poorbeah sepoy, enrolled themselves in the ranks of the British army, and fought faithfully for us to the end of the war. Their help was our safety; without these soldiers, and the assistance rendered by their chieftains, Delhi could never have been taken; while, on the other hand, had they risen and cast in their lot with the mutinous sepoys, no power on earth could have saved us from total annihilation.

The Sikhs are the beau-ideal of soldiers. Tall and erect in bearing, wiry and well-knit, and of great muscular development, their whole appearance stamps them as men who look upon themselves as "lords of the soil," whom it would be difficult to conquer. And without doubt the campaigns of 1845-46 and 1848-49 were the hardest in which we had been engaged in India.

For 100 years they had dominated the land of the Five Rivers. Ever eager for war, their turbulent spirits gave them no rest. It had been a belief that they would in the future acquire the sovereignty of Hindostan, and I know for certain that among the soldiers for many years there had been a tradition that one day they would sack the imperial city of Delhi.

The latter expectation was in a manner fulfilled; but not as an independent nation or under their own leaders did they capture and plunder the Mohammedan capital: they accomplished that feat as loyal subjects of the British Crown.

Every now and then news reached us of the spread of the Mutiny, till from Calcutta to Peshawar there were few stations where the native troops had not joined in the rebellion. Cavalry, infantry, and artillery, all had risen in revolt. The wave of mutiny was surging to and fro throughout the land, and as yet little had been done to stem the tide. True, a small force was being assembled at Umballah, which, under the Commander-in-Chief, was about to march to Delhi, but of the doings of that army we could learn no satisfactory tidings.

The closing days of the month of May passed wearily by, and time hung heavily on our hands. We felt the inevitable reaction from the first few days of excitement, and also missed the comforts and ease to which we had been accustomed in former hot seasons. The barracks were close and stuffy, and the officers, in place of the luxury of their bungalows and their pleasant mess, had to endure privations of every kind.

Hot winds, parching up the already arid ground, blew fiercely every day. At sunset the breeze usually died away; and though the temperature lessened somewhat in degree, we felt a choking sensation from the effects of the dry, still atmosphere. No officer slept in the barrack-room; our servants carried the beds outside, and there, lying down and gasping for breath, we vainly courted the sleep that would not come.

There was, however, a humorous side to this desolate picture, which I must now relate, as it shows that, notwithstanding the state of dejection to which we had been reduced, there still lurked a spirit of fun and mischief among the officers.

For some time after the revolt we had "night-attacks" on the brain. Nothing was spoken of but the chance of our lines being assaulted by wandering bodies of mutinous sepoys. The order-book each evening, reminding us of the danger, inculcated strict vigilance on picket and on guard. So long did this last without any attack being made that the shadowy expectation of what never occurred became our bugbear, a chimera which haunted us night and day.

At last, in a happy hour, it entered into the mind of one of our young Lieutenants, an Irishman, imbued with the spirit of fun, and the jolliest fellow in the regiment, that this illusion under which we were all labouring might be made the subject for a frolic.

He communicated his ideas to myself and some others of the junior officers, and it was then and there decided that, as the sepoys would not attack us, we would create a little excitement and diversion by playing for the nonce the role of mutineers.

The council of war then agreed unanimously that an assault was to be made on the remaining officers when asleep outside the barracks, and that the weapons to be used should be bolsters and pillows.

A certain night was fixed on for the accomplishment of our purpose, and the signal for the attack was to be given by the originator of the plot, who would take upon himself to make sure that the enemy were off their guard, wrapped in the arms of Morpheus.

Everything had been arranged to our satisfaction, and the eventful night came. At ten o'clock lights were put out, and the assaulting party, consisting of six stalwart young subalterns, lay down on their beds outside the barracks, ranged here and there among those who were to play the part of the enemy, and waited for the signal from our commander.

Our opponents seemed to take an unconscionable long time in going to sleep, but at length, in the small hours of the morning, when all was quiet, the "alarm" was sounded in a low whistle.

Jumping up from our beds, each man armed himself with a bolster. In stern and solemn silence our force was marshalled for the attack, and then, without any word of warning, each one began belabouring with all his might the recumbent figures of the foe.

Startled out of their sleep, and in a half-dreamy state of unconsciousness, it may be imagined with what strange feelings they received this assault. Some, more especially the older officers (for in our zeal we spared no one), seemed perfectly bewildered, and in the midst of the shower of blows which rained on them without intermission vowed vengeance and threatened to put us under arrest. We answered them that this was a "night-attack," and they must prepare for defence, as no quarter would be given.

Even the fat and portly Major, notwithstanding his rank, felt the strength of our arms, and, almost bereft of breath between each blow, commanded us to desist. He might as well have spoken to the winds: our blood was up, and the spirit of fun had taken possession, so that I verily believe, had the Colonel or Brigadier been lying there, neither of them would have escaped our onslaught.

The enemy were now fully aroused, and, not relishing the fun of being buffeted unmercifully in their beds without resistance, they one and all turned out and, seizing their pillows, joined in the fight. The attack, begun with tactical judgment, turned now into a confused *mêlée*. Friend and foe were mixed up in one grand shindy, and for many minutes the battle continued without intermission. Blows fell fast and thick; there was a rushing about of half-clad figures swaying bolsters, and each one intent on the same object—namely, that of overcoming his antagonist for the time being. So weird, and yet so utterly ludicrous a sight, surely never has been seen before or since in India.

At length, from sheer exhaustion, the combat came to an end, and, sitting on our beds panting from fatigue, and overcome by the heat of the night, we discussed the incidents of the fight. Some of the senior officers seemed at first inclined to treat the attack as something more than a joke, and threatened to report us to the Colonel. We pointed out to them that such a proceeding would be absurd, for had they not also compromised themselves by joining in the fray? It was not long, however, before they were struck with the grand ridiculousness of this very strange episode; and the question at issue, as may naturally be supposed, ended in laughter. Peace being restored, we wished each other good-night, and, thoroughly worn out by our exertions, all slept soundly till break of day.

The affair was kept quiet as far as possible, but gradually got noised abroad among other regiments of Her Majesty's infantry. Great amusement was caused by the recital, nor for a long period afterwards was the comical "night-attack" at Ferozepore forgotten.

The trial of the sepoys who had been taken prisoners when resisting the detachment sent to disarm them in the fort, and of those also who attacked the arsenal on May 13, had been proceeding for some time. It was a general court-martial composed of thirteen officers, presided over by a Lieutenant-Colonel. Of the prisoners taken, some 100 were singled out as the ringleaders, the rest being put back for trial till a future occasion.

The evidence was most clear as to the heinous offences of mutiny and rebellion with regard to all these men, and they were accordingly found guilty. Sentence was at once pronounced on fourteen of the sepoys, and the punishment was death.

Two men of low caste were to be hanged, while the remaining twelve, comprising Mohammedans and high-caste Hindoos, were to expiate their crime by that most awful and ghastly penalty, execution by being blown to pieces from the mouths of cannons.

This terrible punishment had been but seldom inflicted during British rule in India, the last instance occurring in 1825, when a native regiment mutinied and refused to cross the sea to take part in the first Burmese War.

Neither was it from the English that this special death penalty originated. It had been for hundreds of years the recognized punishment for mutiny and rebellion throughout Hindostan, and in numberless cases was carried out by the Mogul Emperors.

With us at this period it was found necessary to strike terror into the hearts of the rebels, to prove to them that we were resolved at all hazards to crush the revolt, and to give warning that to those who were taken fighting against us no mercy would be shown.

On religious grounds also the infliction of the death penalty by blowing away mutineers at the mouths of cannons was dreaded both by the Hindoos and Mohammedans.

The Hindoo, unless the corpse after death is burnt to ashes with all ceremony, or else consigned to the sacred stream of the Ganges, cannot partake of the glories of the future state, nor dwell in bliss everlasting with the gods of his mythology.

So with the Mohammedan, the Koran enjoins that all

true believers must be buried with the body in the natural state, and only those are exempted who have lost limbs in fighting against the infidel. The joys of Paradise, where ever-young and beautiful houris minister to the wants and pleasures of the faithful, were therefore not for those who met a shameful death and were denied or unable to obtain burial in the orthodox manner.

Thus, it will be seen, the terrors of future shame and dishonour resulted to both Hindoo and Mohammedan by the death we were about to inflict on them; and it was for the awe inspired by the punishment that the military authorities at this time thought proper to carry it out in this unaccustomed manner.

June 13.—The morning of June 13 was fixed upon for the execution. A gallows was erected on the plain to the north side of the fort, facing the native bazaars, and at a distance of some 300 yards. On this two sepoys were to be hanged, and at the same time their comrades in mutiny were to be blown away from guns.

We paraded at daylight every man off duty, and, with the band playing, marched to the place of execution, and drew up in line near the gallows and opposite the native quarter.

Shortly after our arrival the European Light Field Battery, of six guns, appeared on the scene, forming up on our left flank, and about twenty yards in front of the Light Company.

The morning was close and sultry, not a cloud in the sky, and not a breath of wind stirring; and I confess I felt sick with a suffocating sense of horror when I reflected on the terrible sight I was about to witness.

Soon the fourteen mutineers, under a strong escort of our men with fixed bayonets, were seen moving from the fort. They advanced over the plain at our rear, and drew up to the left front of, and at right angles to, the battery of artillery.

I was standing at the extreme right of the line with the Grenadier Company, and some distance from the guns; but I had provided myself with a pair of strong glasses, and therefore saw all that followed clearly and distinctly.

There was no unnecessary delay in the accomplishment of the tragedy. Two of the wretched creatures were marched off to the gallows, and placed with ropes round their necks on a raised platform under the beam.

The order was given for the guns to be loaded, and quick as thought the European artillerymen placed a quarter charge of powder in each piece. The guns were 9-pounders, the muzzles standing about 3 feet from the ground.

During these awful preparations, I watched at intervals the faces of the condemned men, but could detect no traces of fear or agitation in their demeanour. The twelve stood two deep, six in front and six in the rear, calm and undismayed, without uttering a word.

An officer came forward, and, by the Brigadier's order, read the sentence of the court-martial, and at its conclusion the six men in front, under escort, walked towards the battery.

There was a death-like silence over the scene at this time, and, overcome with horror, my heart seemed almost to cease beating.

Arrived at the guns, the culprits were handed over to the artillerymen, who, ready prepared with strong ropes in their hands, seized their victims. Each of these, standing erect, was bound to a cannon and tightly secured, with the small of the back covering the muzzle. And then all at once the silence which reigned around was broken by the oaths and yells of those about to die. These sounds were not uttered by men afraid of death, for they showed the most stoical indifference, but were the long-suppressed utterances of dying souls, who, in the bitterness of their hearts, cursed those who had been instrumental in condemning them to this shameful end. They one and all poured out maledictions on our heads; and in their language, one most rich in expletives, they exhausted the whole vocabulary.

Meanwhile the gunners stood with lighted port-fires, waiting for the word of command to fire the guns and launch the sepoys into eternity.

These were still yelling and raining abuse, some even looking over their shoulders and watching without emotion the port-fires, about to be applied to the touch-holes, when the word "Fire!" sounded from the officer in command, and part of the tragedy was at an end.

A thick cloud of smoke issued from the muzzles of the cannons, through which were distinctly seen by several of us the black heads of the victims, thrown many feet into the air.

While this tragic drama was enacting, the two sepoys to be hanged were turned off the platform.

The artillerymen again loaded the guns, the six remaining prisoners, cursing like their comrades, were bound to them, another discharge, and then an execution, the like of which I hope never to see again, was completed.

All this time a sickening, offensive smell pervaded the air, a stench which only those who have been present at scenes such as these can realize—the pungent odour of burnt human flesh.

The artillerymen had neglected putting up back-boards to their guns, so that, horrible to relate, at each discharge the recoil threw back pieces of burning flesh, bespattering the men and covering them with blood and calcined remains.

A large concourse of natives from the bazaars and city had assembled in front of the houses, facing the guns at a distance, as I said before, of some 300 yards, to watch the execution. At the second discharge of the cannon, and on looking before me, I noticed the ground torn up and earth thrown a slight distance into the air more than 200 paces away. Almost at the same time there was a commotion among the throng in front, some running to and fro, while others ran off in the direction of the houses. I called the attention of an officer who was standing by my side to this strange and unaccountable phenomenon, and said, half joking: "Surely the scattered limbs of the sepoys have not been carried so far?"

He agreed with me that such was impossible; but how to account for the sight we had seen was quite beyond our comprehension.

The drama came to an end about six o'clock, and as is usual, even after a funeral or a military execution, the band struck up an air, and we marched back to barracks, hoping soon to drive from our minds the recollection of the awful scenes we had witnessed.

Two or three hours after our return news arrived that one native had been killed and two wounded among the crowd which had stood in our front, spectators of the recent execution. How this happened has never been explained. At this time a "cantonment guard" was mounted, consisting of a company of European infantry, half a troop of the 10th Light Cavalry, and four guns, and two of these guns loaded with grape were kept ready during the night, the horses being harnessed, etc. Half the cavalry also was held in readiness, saddled; in fact, every precaution was taken to meet an attack.

As far as I can recollect, there were but two executions by blowing away from guns on any large scale by us during the Mutiny; one of them that at Ferozepore.

CHAPTER 2
On the March

After the excitement of the late executions we were
prepared to relapse into our usual state of inaction and
monotony, when, on the morning of June 13, a courier
arrived from Lahore, the headquarters of the Executive
Government of the Punjab. He brought instructions and
orders from Sir John Lawrence to the Brigadier commanding at Ferozepore to the effect that a wing of Her
Majesty's 61st Regiment was to proceed at once to reinforce the army under Sir Henry Barnard, now besieging
the city of Delhi.

That force, on June 8, had fought an action with the
mutineers at Badli-ki-Serai, four miles from Delhi, driving
them from their entrenched position and capturing thirteen guns. The siege of the Mohammedan stronghold had
begun on the next day, but the small band of English, Sikhs,
and Goorkhas which composed the force was quite inadequate to the task entrusted to it, and, in truth, could do
nothing but act on the defensive against the horde of rebellious sepoys, who outnumbered them by four to one.

It may be conceived with what joy the order to advance
was received by the officers and men of my regiment. We
had at length a prospect of entering upon a regular campaign, and the hearts of all of us beat high at the chance of
seeing active service against the enemy.

To the Colonel commanding it was left to select the
five companies composing a wing of the corps to march

to Delhi. All, of course, were eager to go, and we knew there would be heart-burnings and regrets amongst those left behind.

The following companies were chosen out of the ten: Grenadiers, Nos. 2, 3, 7, and the Light Company. They were the strongest in point of numbers in the regiment, and with the fewest men in hospital, so that it could not be said that any favouritism in selection was shown by the Colonel. The wing numbered, all told, including officers and the band, 450 men—a timely reinforcement, which, together with the same number of Her Majesty's 8th Foot from Jullundur, would increase materially the army before Delhi.

No time was lost in making preparations for the march. Our camp equipage was ready at hand, a sufficient number of elephants, camels, and oxen were easily procured from the commissariat authorities, and by eight o'clock that evening we were on our way.

In those days a European regiment on the line of march in India presented a striking scene. Each corps had its own quota of camp-followers, numbering in every instance more than the regiment itself, so that transport was required for fully 2,000 souls, and often when moving along the road the baggage-train extended a mile in length. The camp, when pitched, covered a large area of ground. Everything was regulated with the utmost order, and the positions of the motley group were defined to a nicety.

We had been directed to take as small a kit as possible, each officer being limited to two camels to carry his tent and personal effects. Our native servants accompanied us on the line of march, and I must here mention that during the long campaign on which we were about to enter there was not one single instance of desertion among these faithful and devoted followers.

Everything being ready, we paraded a little before sunset on the evening of June 13. The terrible heat which prevailed at this time of the year prevented us from marching during the day-time. Moreover, it was necessary to preserve the health of the soldiers at this critical period, when every European in India was required to make head against the rebels. So on every occasion when practicable the English regiments moving over the country marched at night, resting under cover of their tents during the day.[1]

Shortly after sunset, we bade *adieu* (an eternal one, alas! for many of the gallant souls assembled) to the comrades we were leaving behind; the band struck up, and we set off in high spirits on our long and arduous march of more than 350 miles.

The night, as usual, was close and sultry, with a slight hot wind blowing; but the men stepped out briskly, the soldiers of the leading company presently striking up a well-known song, the chorus of which was joined in by the men in the rear. We marched slowly, for it was necessary every now and then to halt so as to allow the long train of baggage to come up; and it was nearly sunrise before we reached the first halting-ground. The camp was pitched, and we remained under cover all day, starting, as before, soon after sunset.

And thus passed the sixteen days which were occupied in reaching Delhi. Every precaution was taken to prevent surprise, as we were marching, to all intents and purposes, through an enemy's country, and expected attacks on our baggage from straggling bodies of mutineers.

June 18.—At Loodianah, five marches from Ferozepore, and which we reached on June 18, we were fortunate enough to find more comfortable quarters, the men moving into some of the buildings which had formerly been occupied by Her Majesty's 50th Regiment, the officers living in the Kacherri.

1: The heat even under such cover was intense, averaging 115° Fahr.

Here, behind *tatties* and under *punkas*, and with iced drinks, we were able to keep pretty cool; but, sad to say, soon after our arrival in the station that terrible scourge cholera broke out in our ranks, and in a few hours six men succumbed to this frightful malady. On every succeeding day men were attacked and died, so that, unhappily, up to July 1 we lost in all thirty gallant fellows.

This disease never left us during the entire campaign; upwards of 250 soldiers of my regiment fell victims to the destroyer; nor were we entirely free from it till the end of the year. Many more were attacked, who recovered, but were debarred through excessive weakness from serving in the ranks, and were invalided home.

June 23.—On reaching Umballah, we found the station all but deserted, nearly all the European troops having been sent on to join the Delhi force. The church had been placed in a state of defence, all its walls loopholed, and around it had been constructed a work consisting of a wall and parapet, with towers of brickwork armed with field-pieces *en barbette* at the angles.

In it were quartered some of the 1st Bengal Fusiliers, lately brought down from Dagshai. About ninety of these marched with us to Delhi. Here also we were joined by four officers of the (late) 57th Native Infantry, who had received orders to join our wing, eventually to fill up vacancies in the native corps on reaching the scene of operations. With these we were in all twenty-four officers—rather a strong complement even for a whole regiment.

The concluding days of the march were trying in the extreme. Weary and footsore, and often parched with thirst, we tramped along the hot and dusty roads, often for miles up to our ankles in deep sand. We were so tired and overcome with want of rest that many of us actually fell fast asleep along the road, and would be rudely awakened by falling against others who were in the same plight as ourselves. At midnight we rested, when coffee and refreshment were served out to the officers and men. The halt sounded every hour, and for five minutes we threw ourselves down on the hard ground or on the hot sand and at once fell asleep, waking up somewhat restored to continue our toilsome journey.

From Jugraon onward we had rather long marches, and it was considered advisable to convey the men part of the way in hackeries; the arrangement being that they should march halfway, then halt for coffee and refreshment, and afterwards ride the remainder of the distance.

By this means they were kept fresh for the work before them, which, we had every reason to believe, would be anything but light. At Umballah I took the opportunity of calling on my friend Mr. George Barnes, the Commissioner of the Cis-Sutlej States. He had shown me boundless hospitality, and was like a father to me when I joined my regiment as a lad at Kussowlie. A man of great intellectual attainments and sound judgment, he was an honour to the Bengal Civil Service. There was no officer at that momentous period in whom Sir John Lawrence placed more confidence. His familiarity with the native character, and the friendship borne towards him by the Sikh chieftains, enabled him throughout the Siege of Delhi to keep open communication with the Punjab, and supply the force with stores, provisions, and ammunition. He would, without doubt, have risen to the highest honours in his profession had he not been stricken with a fatal illness in 1859, when holding the responsible post of Foreign Secretary to the Government of India.

A few marches from Delhi we passed over the historic field of Paniput, where three sanguinary battles had been fought in different ages, each deciding the fate of Hindostan for the time being. More than 100,000 men had been slain in these actions, and we felt we were marching over ground the dust of which was thickly permeated with the ashes of human beings.

Here first we heard the sound of distant cannonades, borne thus far to our ears by the stillness of the night—a sound which told us that our comrades before Delhi were still holding their position against the enemy.

At length, on July 1, just as the sun was rising, we emerged from a forest of trees on to the plain over which the army under Sir Henry Barnard had moved on June 8 to attack the entrenchments of the mutineers at Badli-ki-Serai.

July 1.—Eagerly we cast our eyes over the ground to our front, and with pride in our hearts thought of that gallant little force which had advanced across this plain on that eventful morn under a terrific fire from the enemy's guns.

Soon we reached the entrenchments which had been thrown up by the rebels to bar the progress of our soldiers, and, lying in all directions, we saw numerous skeletons of men and horses, the bones already bleached to whiteness from the effects of the burning sun. Dead bodies of camels and oxen were also strewn about, and the stench was sickening. We were now about four miles from Delhi, and were met by a squadron of the 6th Carabineers, sent to escort us into camp. They received us with a shout of welcome, and, while we halted for a short time, inquiries were made as to the incidents of the siege.

We learnt that our small army, with the tenacity of a bulldog, was holding its own on the ridge overlooking the city, that sorties by the rebels were of almost daily and nightly occurrence, and that the losses on our side were increasing.

With the Carabineers in our front, the march was continued, the white tents of the besieging force appearing in sight about eight o'clock. Then the band struck up "Cheer, boys, cheer!" and, crossing the canal by a bridge, we entered the camp.

Crowds of soldiers, European as well as native, stalwart Sikhs and Punjabees, came down to welcome us on our arrival, the road on each side being lined with swarthy, sun-burnt, and already war-worn men. They cheered us to the echo, and in their joy rushed amongst our ranks, shaking hands with both officers and men.

CHAPTER 3
Before Delhi

A situation had already been marked out for our en-
campment, and, directed by an officer, we passed through
the main portion of our lines, and halted at the bottom of
the ridge on the extreme left of our position. Some time
was occupied after the arrival of the baggage in pitching
our camp; but when all was concluded, Vicars and I started
on foot to take our first view of the imperial city.

We walked a short distance to the right, and along the
foot of the ridge, and then ascended, making our way to
the celebrated Flagstaff Tower. We mounted to the top: and
shall I ever forget the sight which met our gaze?

About a mile to our front, and stretching to right and
left as far as the eye could reach, appeared the high walls
and the bastions of Delhi. The intervening space below was
covered with a thick forest of trees and gardens, forming
a dense mass of verdure, in the midst of which, and peep-
ing out here and there in picturesque confusion, were the
white walls and roofs of numerous buildings. Tall and grace-
ful minarets, Hindoo temples and Mohammedan mosques,
symmetrical in shape and gorgeous in colouring, appeared
interspersed in endless numbers among the densely-packed
houses inside the city, their domes and spires shining with
a brilliant radiance, clear-cut against the sky. Above all, in
the far distance towered the Jama Masjid, or Great Mosque,
its three huge domes of pure white marble, with two high
minarets, dwarfing into insignificance the buildings by

which it was surrounded—surely, the noblest work of art ever built by man for the service of the Creator.

To the left could be seen the lofty castellated walls of the Palace of the Emperors, the former seat of the Great Mogul—that palace in which at that moment the degenerate descendant of Timour, and last representative of his race, held his court, and in his pride of heart fondly hoped that British rule was at an end.

Beyond rose the ancient fortress of Selimgarh, its walls, as well as those of the palace on the north side, washed by the waters of the Jumna. A long bridge of boats connected the fort with the opposite bank of the river, here many hundred yards in width: and over this we could see, with the aid of glasses, bodies of armed men moving.

It was by this bridge that most of the reinforcements and all the supplies for the mutineers crossed over to the city. On the very day of our arrival the mutinous Bareilly Brigade of infantry and artillery, numbering over 3,000 men, marched across this bridge. Our advanced picket at the Metcalfe House stables, close to the Jumna, heard distinctly their bands playing "Cheer, boys, cheer!" the very same tune with which we had celebrated our entrance into camp that morning.

Few cities in the world have passed through such vicissitudes as Delhi. Tradition says it was the capital of an empire ages before the great Macedonian invaded India, and its origin is lost in the mists of antiquity. Traces there were in every direction, amid the interminable cluster of ruins and mounds outside the present city, of cities still more vast, the builders and inhabitants of which lived before the dawn of history.

Delhi had been taken and sacked times out of number. Its riches were beyond compare; and for hundreds of years it had been the prey, not only of every conqueror who invaded India from the north-west, but also of every race which, during the perpetual wars in Hindostan, happened for the time to be predominant. Tartars, Turks, Afghans, Persians, Mahrattas and Rajpoots, each in turn in succeeding ages had been masters of the city. There had been indiscriminate massacres of the populace, the last by Nadir Shah, the King of Persia in 1747, when 100,000 souls were put to death by his order, and booty to a fabulous amount was carried away. Still, notwithstanding the vicissitudes of fortune through which it had passed, Delhi was, in 1857, one of the largest, most beautiful, and certainly the richest city in Hindostan. We knew well that there was wealth untold within the walls, and our hearts were cheered even at this time when we thought of the prize-money which would fall to our share at the capture of the rebellious city.

The walls surrounding Delhi were seven miles in circumference, flanked at intervals by strong bastions, on which the enemy had mounted the largest guns and mortars, procured from the arsenal. Munitions of war they had in abundance—enough to last them, at the present rate of firing, for nearly three years. Long we gazed, fascinated at the scene before us. A dead silence had reigned for some time, when we were awakened from our dreams by the whiz and hissing of a shell fired by the enemy. It fell close below the tower and burst without doing any harm; but some jets of smoke appeared on the bastions of the city, and shells and round-shot fired at the ridge along the crest of which a small body of our men was moving. The cannonade lasted for some time, our own guns replying at intervals. We could plainly see the dark forms of the rebel artillerymen, stripped to the waist, sponging and firing with great rapidity, their shot being chiefly directed at the three other buildings on the ridge—namely, the Observatory— the Mosque, as it was called—and, on the extreme right, Hindoo Rao's house.

From the Flagstaff Tower the ridge trended in a southerly direction towards those buildings, approaching gradually nearer and nearer to the city, till at Hindoo Rao's house it was distant about 1,200 yards from the walls.

To the rear of this ridge, and some distance below, so that all view of Delhi was quite shut out from it, was the camp of the besieging army, numbering at this period about 6,000 men. The tents were pitched at regular intervals behind the ruined houses of the old cantonment, which, at the outbreak on May 11, had been burnt and destroyed by the sepoys. A canal which supplied us with water from the Jumna ran round the ridge past the suburb of Kishenganj into the city, and was crossed by two bridges, over which communication with the country to the north-west, and leading to the Punjab, was kept open by the loyal Sikh chieftains and their retainers.

Our position on the ridge extended about a mile and a half, the right and left front flanks defended by outlying advanced pickets, which I shall hereafter describe.

The city walls, as before recorded, were seven miles in circumference, so that at this time, and, in fact, almost to the end of the siege, we, with our small force, in a manner only commanded a small part of the city. The bridge of boats remained to the last in the possession of the enemy, and was quite out of range even from our advanced approaches, while to the right and rear of the city the gates gave full ingress to reinforcing bodies of insurgents from the south, whose entrance we were unable to prevent.

Our investment, if such it could be called, was therefore only partial, being confined to that portion of the city extending from the water battery near Selimgarh Fort to the Ajmir Gate, which was just visible from the extreme right of the ridge. This part was defended by, I think, four bastions, named, respectively, the Water, Kashmir, Mori, and Burn. Three gates besides the Lahore gave egress to the mutineers when making sorties, the afterwards celebrated Kashmir Gate, the Kabul and the Ajmir Gates.

The Hindoo Rao's house, on the right of the ridge where it sloped down into the plain, was the key of our position, and was defended with great bravery and unflinching tenacity throughout the whole siege by the Sirmoor battalion of Goorkhas, and portions of the 60th Royal Rifles and the Guide Corps. Incessant day and night attacks were here made by the enemy, who knew that, were that position turned, our camp—in fact, our very existence as a besieging force—would be imperilled.

But no assault, however strong and determined, made any impression on the men of these gallant regiments, led by Major Reid, the officer commanding the Sirmoor battalion. They lost in killed and wounded a number far out of all proportion to that of any other corps before Delhi, and must in truth be reckoned the heroes of the siege.

The Goorkhas are recruited in the mountain districts of the Himalayas, in the kingdom of Nepal. They are short and squat in figure, never more than five feet three inches in height, of dark complexion, with deep-set eyes and high cheek-bones denoting their affinity to the Turanian race. Good-humoured and of a cheerful disposition, they have always been great favourites with the European soldiers, whose ways and peculiarities they endeavour to imitate to a ludicrous extent. In battle, as I have often seen them, they seem in their proper element, fierce and courageous, shrinking from no danger. They carried, besides the musket, a short, heavy, curved knife called a *kukri*, a formidable weapon of which the sepoys were in deadly terror. As soldiers they are second to none, amenable to discipline and docile, but very tigers when roused; they fought with unflinching spirit during the Mutiny, freely giving up their lives in the service of their European masters.

And now that I have endeavoured, for the purposes of this narrative, to explain our position and that of the enemy, I shall proceed to recount, as far as my recollection serves, the main incidents of the siege, and more particularly those in which I personally took part.

The camp of my regiment was pitched, as I have said, on the extreme left of the besieging force, on the rear slope of the ridge. We were completely hidden from any view of the city, and but for the sound of the firing close by, which seldom ceased day or night, might have fancied ourselves far away from Delhi.

Cholera still carried off its victims from our midst, and the very night of our arrival I performed the melancholy duty of reading the Burial Service over five gallant fellows of the Grenadier Company who had died that day from the fell disease.

The heat was insupportable, the thermometer under the shade of my tent marking 112°F.; and to add to our misery there came upon us a plague of flies, the like of which I verily believe had not been on the earth since Moses in that manner brought down the wrath of God on the Egyptians. They literally darkened the air, descending in myriads and covering everything in our midst. Foul and loathsome they were, and we knew that they owed their existence to, and fattened on, the putrid corpses of dead men and animals which lay rotting and unburied in every direction. The air was tainted with corruption, and the heat was intense. Can it, then, be wondered that pestilence increased daily in the camp, claiming its victims from every regiment, native as well as European?

About this time many spies were captured and executed; in fact, so many prisoners were taken by the pickets that it was ordered that for the future, instead of being sent under escort to the camp for trial, they should be summarily dealt with by the officers commanding pickets.

On the evening of July 2 I was sent, in command of fifty men, to relieve the picket at a place called the "Cow House"; this was an outshed belonging to Sir Theophilus

Metcalfe's mansion, burnt by the rebels on May 11, and midway between that building and the stables, at each of which were stationed 150 men. At the beginning of the siege our left advanced flank, on the side of the River Jumna, was exposed to constant attacks by the enemy, and the three pickets mentioned above had been since that time stationed at those places. Each communicated with the other, the one to the right being on a mound near the ruins of the house, and some 1,200 yards from the city, the cowshed situated midway between this mound and the river, and, lastly, the stables close to the banks, all partially hidden from view of the batteries on the walls by gardens and thick clusters of trees.

I stationed my men at the sheds, and placed double rows of sentries to my front along the edge of a deep *nullah*, or ravine.

Soon after this that gallant officer, Lieutenant Hodson (on whose memory lately aspersions have been cast by an author who knows nothing of the subject on which he has written), rode up to the picket and told me that a sortie in force was expected that night, and that I was to keep a sharp lookout to prevent surprise.

Hodson, besides commanding a regiment of native Sikh cavalry of his own raising, was head of the Intelligence Department. He covered himself with glory during the siege, was untiring in his exertions and well-nigh ubiquitous, riding incessantly round the pickets at night, and being present at most of the engagements. He was a perfect Hindustani scholar, and it was reported in camp, though with what truth I cannot say, that he on several occasions entered Delhi in disguise during the siege to gain information of the enemy's intentions. This may have been exaggeration, but it is nevertheless certain that, through some source or other, he made himself well acquainted with the doings and movements of the mutineers.

Shortly after he left, the field-officer on duty appeared, who ordered me, in case I should be attacked, to defend my post to the last extremity, and in no case to fall back, adding that to my picket, and to those on my right and left, the safety of the camp during the expected sortie, together with the security of our left flank, was entrusted.

After darkness set in the enemy commenced a furious cannonade in the direction of the three pickets, round shot whistling through the trees and shells bursting around us. The din and roar were deafening, but firing, as they did, at random, little damage was done. Nothing can be grander than the sight of live shells cleaving the air on a dark night. They seemed like so many brilliant meteors rushing through the heavens, or like lightning-flashes during a storm, and this being my first experience of the sort, no words can paint my awe and admiration.

We naturally expected an attack in force from the insurgents under cover of the cannonade; but hours passed by in suspense and anxiety, and none was attempted. The firing was continued all night—sleep being impossible—and ceased only at daybreak, when the relief arrived, and I marched the picket back to our camp.

July 3.—That day the monsoon—the Indian wet season—set in, and rain descended in sheets of water for many hours.

In the afternoon it was reported that a large force of mutineers was moving out of the city by the Kabul and Ajmir Gates into the suburbs to the right front of our position, and the alarm sounded, most of the troops in camp turning out and assembling on the road to the rear of the canal. Here we were halted for some time, it being uncertain what direction had been taken by the enemy.

At sunset two *doolies*, escorted by men of the 5th Punjab Cavalry, were seen on the road coming towards us. They contained the bodies of a European sergeant and a man of the Road Department, who had been surprised and cut to pieces by some of the rebel cavalry. The escort also reported that a body of insurgents numbering many thousand men had been seen moving towards Alipore, one march in our rear, their object, it was supposed, being to cut off supplies and intercept treasure.

It being too late to start in pursuit of the enemy, we were dismissed to our quarters, being warned to hold ourselves in readiness to turn out at a moment's notice.

July 4.—That night the sound of the enemy's guns to our rear was heard in the camp, and soon after 2 a. m. we paraded, and joined a force destined to overtake or cut off the mutineers on their return to Delhi. The little army, consisting of 1,500 men, cavalry, artillery, and infantry, marched at once towards Alipore. After we had proceeded three miles, and just at daybreak, news was brought that the enemy, after plundering the town, were retreating to the city laden with booty.

Major Coke, who was in command, then changed our direction to the left, and we advanced for about two miles over swampy ground to a canal, the cavalry being in front, then the infantry, the battery of Horse Artillery bringing up the rear.

When near the canal, which was shaded on each side by trees, the Major advanced to reconnoitre, and on his return, the order was given, "Guns to the front!" The Horse Artillery galloped past us, and we then heard that the enemy were in sight on the other side of the canal.

Crossing a bridge, and passing through trees and jungle, the whole force debouched on an open plain, and formed in order of battle. The first line consisted of the artillery, in the centre, flanked on each side by the cavalry. The mounted force consisted of portions of the 9th Lancers, the Carabineers, and that fine regiment, the Guide Corps. Coke's Corps of Punjabees and my regiment formed the second line.

It was a pretty sight to see this miniature army advancing

in perfect order towards the enemy. The plain extended for a mile quite open and without trees, bounded at that distance by a village, in which the insurgent guns were posted. Clouds of horsemen, apparently without any formation, hovered on each side of the village, and a large force of infantry was standing in line somewhat in advance.

Our guns came into action at a distance of about 1,000 yards from the village, and were soon answered by those of the enemy, their shot striking unpleasantly close to our line, and ricochetting over our heads. Still we advanced, hoping that the rebels would stand till we came to close quarters. At 500 yards the fire from our artillery seemed to prove too hot for them; and presently, to our infinite disgust, we saw their infantry moving off to the left, followed shortly after by the cavalry. Then their guns ceased firing, and were also quickly withdrawn.

The Carabineers and Guides were sent in pursuit, and cut up some stragglers; but the insurgents stampeded at a great pace, and succeeded in carrying off all their guns.

A few sepoys were found hiding in the village huts, and were killed by our men, the Alipore plunder was recovered, besides some ammunition and camp equipment, and, rather dissatisfied with the result of the action, we moved slowly back across the plain.

The regiment was commanded on this occasion by our senior Captain, an officer of some thirty-five years' service. He was, without exception, the greatest oddity for a soldier that our army has ever seen. Five feet two inches in height, with an enormous head, short, hunchback body, long arms, and thin, shrivelled legs, his whole appearance reminded one of Dickens' celebrated character Quilp, in the "Old Curiosity Shop." Entering the service in the "good" old times, when there was no examination by a medical man, he had, through some back-door influence, obtained a commission in the army. All his service had been passed abroad, exchanging from one regiment to another, for it would have been utterly impossible for him to have retained his commission in England. Marching, he was unable to keep step with the men, and on horseback he presented the most ludicrous appearance, being quite unable to ride, and looking more like a monkey than a human being. On our first advance across the plain the little Captain was riding in our front, vainly endeavouring to make his horse move faster, and striking him every now and then on the flanks with his sword. I was on the right of the line, and, together with the men, could not keep from laughing, when a friend of mine—a tall officer of one of the native infantry regiments—rode to my side and asked me who that was leading the regiment. I answered, "He is our commanding officer."

The sun shone with intense heat on our march back across the plain, and the European soldiers began to feel its effects, many being struck down with apoplexy. About midday the infantry halted at the canal, the guns and most of the cavalry returning to camp, as it was supposed there would be no more work for them to do. We lay down in the welcome shade of the trees on the bank, enjoying our breakfast, which had been brought to us by our native servants, and, in company with an officer of the 9th Lancers, I was discussing a bottle of ale, the sweetest draught I think I have ever tasted. The arms were piled in our front, and at intervals we watched, as they crossed the canal, a troop of elephants which had been sent out to bring the sick and wounded into camp.

All at once, from our left front, and without any warning, shots came whistling through the trees and jungle, and some men lying on the ground were hit. The regiment at once fell in and changed front to the left, moving in the direction from which the shots were coming.

Frightened at the sound of the firing, the elephants were

seized with a panic and made off across the canal. Trumpeting, with their trunks high above their heads, they floundered through the water to the opposite side, their drivers vainly attempting to stop their flight. We saw them disappearing through the trees, and learnt afterwards that they never stopped till close to their own quarters at the camp.

Meanwhile the shots came thick and fast, and we advanced in line till we came to a comparatively open space, and in sight of the enemy—a large body of infantry outnumbering us by four to one. They were at no great distance from us, and a sharp musketry fire was kept up from both sides, causing heavy losses.

Seeing that no object was to be gained with our small force by encountering one so vastly superior, Major Coke deemed it prudent to retire, and retreating firing, we crossed the bridge and lined the bank on each side.

The enemy followed, their men forming opposite to us and keeping up a steady fire at a distance of from 100 to 150 yards. I was on the right of the line with the Grenadiers, when, half an hour later, I was directed by the Adjutant to march my men to the left of the bridge to reinforce the Light Company, who were being hard pressed by the insurgents, some of whom were wading through the canal, with the evident intention of turning our left flank. We crept along under the bank, and were received with joy by our comrades, one of them, I well remember, welcoming us in most forcible language, and intimating that they would soon have been sent to **** if we had not come.

The file-firing here was continuous, a perfect hail of bullets, and it was dangerous to show one's head over the bank. Shouting and taunting us, the rebels came up close to the opposite side, and were struck down in numbers by our men, who rested their muskets on the bank and took sure aim. Still, the contest was most unequal; the enemy were wading in force through the water on our left, and the day would have gone hard with us from their overwhelming numerical superiority, when, just at this critical moment, the galloping of horses and the noise of wheels was heard in our rear.

Six Horse Artillery guns, led by Major Tombs—one of the most gallant officers in camp—came thundering along the road. They passed with a cheer, crossed the bridge at full speed, wheeled to their left, unlimbered as quick as lightning, and opened fire on the rebels. Taken completely by surprise, these made no stand, and fled pell-mell towards Delhi, leaving altogether 200 dead on the ground.

It was now nearly five o'clock, and we were distant four miles from camp. Many of our men had died from apoplexy and sunstroke, their faces turning quite black in a few minutes—a horrible sight. These, with the killed and the sick and wounded, were placed on the backs of a fresh lot of elephants, which had just arrived; and, scarcely able to drag one leg after the other, we turned our faces towards the camp, reaching our own quarters soon after sunset.

This was a terrible and trying day for all engaged, and more especially for the European infantry. We had been under arms for seventeen hours, most of the time exposed to the pitiless rays of an Indian sun, under fire for a considerable period, and, with the exception of the slight halt for breakfast, on our feet all the time.

When nearing camp we were met by the General, Sir Henry Barnard, who addressed us with some kindly words, and little did we think that that was the last occasion we should see the gallant old soldier. The following morning he was attacked with cholera, and expired in the afternoon, deeply regretted by the whole army.

No man could possibly have been placed in a more trying situation than he who had just given up his life in the service of his country. Called on to command an army to which was entrusted the safety of British rule in India, the cares and anxiety of the task, together with his unremitting attention to his duties and constant exposure to the sun, made him peculiarly susceptible to the disease from which he died. He had served with distinction in the Crimean campaign, and had only landed in India to take command of a division in the April of this year.

July 5.—From July 5 to 8 nothing of note occurred. The enemy kept up, as usual, a constant fire upon the ridge and outlying pickets; but no attempt at a sortie was made.

I visited the Flagstaff Tower each day when off duty, seemingly never tired of gazing at the glorious panorama spread out before me, and watching the batteries delivering their unceasing fire.

With the exception of two 24-pound cannon taken from the enemy, for which we had no shot, the heaviest guns on the ridge were 18-pounders and a few small mortars. Having possession of the great arsenal, the insurgents mounted on the bastions of Delhi 32-and 24-pounder guns and 13-inch mortars, their trained artillerymen acquitting themselves right valiantly, and making excellent practice. They were almost to a man killed at their guns during the siege, and towards the end the difference in firing was fully perceptible, when the infantry filled their places and worked the guns.

Having no round-shot for the two 24-pounders, we were reduced to firing back on the city the shot of the same calibre hurled against us, and a reward of half a rupee per shot was paid by the commissariat to any camp-follower bringing in the missiles.

On one occasion I saw a party of native servants, carrying on their heads cooked provisions for the men on picket, wend their way up the slope from the camp. Two round-shot fired by the enemy struck the top of the ridge and rolled down the declivity. Here was a prize worth contending for, and the cooks, depositing the dishes on the ground, ran in all haste to seize the treasures. I watched the race with interest, and anticipated some fun, knowing that in their eagerness they would forget that the shots had not had time to cool. Two men in advance of the rest picked up the balls, and, uttering a cry, dropped them quickly, rubbing and blowing their hands. The remainder stood patiently waiting, and then, after a time, spent evidently in deliberation, two men placed the shot on their heads, and all in a body moved off towards the commissariat quarters to receive and divide the reward.

July 7.—On the morning of July 7, I accompanied a detachment of 150 men under command of a Captain to relieve the picket at the mound close to the ruins of Sir Theophilus Metcalfe's house. This mansion, built by the present baronet's father, was situated about 1,200 yards from the walls of the city, and surrounded by trees and gardens. At the outbreak of May 11, it had been plundered and burnt by the mutinous sepoys and *badmashes*, who also in like manner had destroyed every house belonging to the Europeans in the suburbs of Delhi and the adjoining cantonment. Of the murders that then took place I shall have something to say hereafter, when writing the history of a young schoolfellow whose sister was killed by the insurgents.

From our position on picket we could see a short distance in front, the ground having been partially cleared of trees and undergrowth. A chain of double sentries was posted, and the utmost vigilance observed. We could hear the batteries opening on the ridge, while occasionally, as if to harass the picket, a 13-inch shell would burst either in our front or in our rear. The night passed quickly, and at daybreak, when visiting the sentries, I heard distinctly the bugles of the rebels sounding the reveille, succeeded by other familiar calls. It seemed strange to hear our own bugle-calls sounded by men who were now our enemies; and not only was this the case, but also the insurgents for some time wore the scarlet uniform of the British soldiers, and invariably to the end of the war gave the English words of command they had been taught in our service.

We were relieved from picket on the morning of the 8th, and returned to our camp, remaining quiet during the day. Executions by hanging took place every day, but after the first horrible experience nothing would induce me to be a spectator. The rain, which had begun on the 3rd, continued almost without intermission, our camp becoming a quagmire, and the muggy, moist atmosphere increasing the ravages of cholera amongst our unfortunate soldiers.

July 9.—At sunrise on the 9th, a terrific cannonade woke us out of our sleep; but, the main camp being some distance from the right of the ridge, we for a long time heard no tidings of what was going on. At 8 a. m. the bugles of the regiments on the right sounded the alarm, followed at once by the "assembly."

Some 200 men of my regiment, all that remained off duty, paraded in front of the tents, and received orders to march to the centre rear of the camp, in rear of the quarters of the General in command. Here we were joined by some companies of the 8th Regiment and a battalion of Sikhs, and, continuing our march, we halted near the tents of Tombs' battery of Horse Artillery.

Lying around and even among the tent-ropes were dead bodies of the enemy's cavalry, and a little way beyond, close to the graveyard, some men of the 75th were firing into the branches of the trees which surrounded the enclosure. Every now and then the body of a rebel would fall on the ground at their feet, the soldiers laughing and chatting together, and making as much sport out of the novel business as though they were shooting at birds in the branches of a tree.

How the native cavalry came there was at first inexplicable to us; but we were informed afterwards that a body of irregular horsemen, dressed in white, the same uniform as that worn by the 9th Irregulars on our side, had, with the greatest daring, an hour before dashed across the canal bridge and charged the picket of the Carabineers, making also for the two guns of Tombs' battery. The former, mostly young soldiers, had turned and fled, all save their officer and one sergeant, who nobly stood their ground. Lieutenant Hills, who commanded the two guns on picket, also alone charged the horsemen, cutting down one or two of the sowars.

Meantime the guns were unlimbered, but before they had time to fire, the enemy were upon them. Hills was struck down badly wounded, and was on the point of being despatched by a sowar, when Major Tombs, hearing the noise, rushed out of his tent, and seeing the plight his subaltern was in, fired his revolver at thirty yards and killed the sowar.

The camp was now fairly alarmed; the guns of Olpherts' battery opened on the enemy, and, some men of the 75th appearing on the scene, the rebels were shot down in every direction, thirty-five being killed, and the rest escaping by the bridge. A few climbed into the trees and were shot down as I have said before.

This attack by the enemy's cavalry was a fitting prelude to the events of the memorable sortie of that day.

At early morn, under cover of an unceasing cannonade from the city batteries on to the right of our position, the insurgents in great force and of all arms streamed out from the gates, making in the direction of the suburb of Kishenganj, their evident intention being to turn our right flank and make for our camp.

Seeing that the enemy were increasing in numbers, and coming on with great determination, the alarm had sounded; and detachments from most of the regiments, with Horse Artillery and a few cavalry under the command of Brigadier-General Chamberlain, marched towards the right rear of the camp, taking the road to the suburb of Kishenganj.

We crossed the canal at about 10 a. m., and, moving in column for some little distance, came in sight of advanced bodies of the enemy, chiefly infantry with cavalry and field artillery on each flank. We formed in line, sending out skirmishers, the guns opened fire—the country here being pretty open—and the action began.

Soon we drove back the rebels, who continued retreating in excellent order, turning at intervals and discharging their muskets, while every now and then their guns were faced about and unlimbered, and round-shot and grape sent among our ranks. As we advanced, the vegetation became thicker, and we were confronted at times by high hedges of prickly-pear and cactus, growing so close together that it was impossible to make our way through. This occasioned several détours, the sepoys lining the hedges and firing at us through loopholes and openings, cursing the *gore log*[1] and daring us to come on.

The rain, which had kept off during the morning, now descended in a steady downpour, soaking through our thin cotton clothing, and in a few minutes drenching us to the skin.

Passing the obstacles on each flank, the force again formed in as good order as the inequalities of the ground would permit, and continued its advance, all the time under a heavy fire of artillery and musketry. We caught glimpses of the enemy retreating towards the Kishenganj Serai, but the vegetation was so dense in the numerous gardens, and the view so obstructed by stone walls and ruined buildings, that it was with great difficulty that we made any progress, nor, having the advantage of so much cover, did the enemy suffer much loss from our musketry fire.

1: White people.

Many of our men fell at this period of the fight; despising the enemy and refusing to take cover, our soldiers would stand out exposed and deliver their fire, offering a sure aim to the enemy's marksmen. It was a continual rush from one point to another, halting and firing at intervals, the rebels all the time slowly retreating. Our Horse Artillery at this juncture could only act on occasions, the ground being so broken that the guns were often brought to a standstill.

All this time the batteries on the ridge, which from their high position could see what was going on, sent shells and round-shot at every opportunity over our heads, dispersing the mutineers when grouped together in any large number, and dealing death amongst them.

We saw them lying in heaps of twenty and thirty as we advanced, and the fire was so hot and the practice so excellent that the enemy evacuated the gardens and fled towards the suburb of Kishenganj.

Here the country was more open, so, re-forming our scattered line, with skirmishers in advance, we drove the rebels before us, the Horse Artillery playing on them in the open and bringing down scores.

Crossing the canal (which here barred our progress) by a bridge, we entered into a wide lane to the left, the high bank of the canal being on one side and the walls of a large caravanserai on the other.

The insurgents were posted at the far end of the lane, where it opened out at the gate of the *serai*, and received us, as we advanced at the double, with a rattling fire of musketry. Some climbed to the top of the bank, while others fired down at us from the walls. It was a perfect *feu d'enfer*, and the loss on our side became so heavy that a temporary check was the result, and it was only with great trouble that the men could be urged on.

Seeing a disposition to waver, Colonel W. Jones, the Brigadier under Chamberlain, with great bravery placed himself in front on foot, and called on the soldiers, now a confused mass of Sikhs, Goorkhas, and Europeans, to charge and dislodge the enemy from the end of the lane. He was answered with a ringing cheer, the men broke into a run, and, without firing a shot, charged the sepoys, who waited till we were within fifty yards, and then, as usual, turned and fled.

Some entered the *caravanserai* by the large gate, which they attempted to shut; but we were too quick for them, and following close on their heels, a hard fight began in the enclosure.

Others of the enemy ran onwards in the direction of the city, chased by portions of our force, who pursued them a long distance, and after a desperate resistance killed many who in their flight had taken refuge in the *serais* and buildings.

The party I was with in the great *caravanserai* ranged the place like demons, the English soldiers putting to death every sepoy they could find. Their aspect was certainly inhuman—eyes flashing with passion and revenge, faces wet and blackened from powder through biting cartridges; it would have been useless to attempt to check them in their work of slaughter.

Twenty or more of the insurgents, flying for life from their pitiless foe, made for a small building standing in the centre of the serai. They were followed by our men, who entered after them at the door. The house had four windows, one on each side, about three feet from the ground, and I ran to one and looked in.

The wretched fugitives had thrown down their arms and, crouching on the floor with their backs to the wall, begged with out-stretched hands for mercy, calling out in their language, "*Dohai! dohai!*" words I well knew the meaning of, and which I had often heard under similar circumstances. I knew, however, that no quarter would be given, and in a short time every rebel lay in the agonies of death.

Most of the force, as I have related, had continued chasing the enemy, so that for some time we were alone and few in number in the serai. It was nearly five o'clock, and we thought that, as far as we were concerned, the action was over.

It was not so, however. Shouts and yells were heard outside, and, running to see, we found a fresh force of the mutineers assembled outside the gates. There was nothing for it but to make a rush and fight our way through; so with fixed bayonets we charged through them, meeting soon afterwards the remainder of the force on its way back. Joining with these, we drove the enemy again before us till we came within 700 yards of the city walls, there losing sight of our foes. Their guns fired into us, but the insurgent infantry seemed now to have had sufficient fighting for one day, and not one man was to be seen.

Our work was accomplished, and the order was given to retire. Slowly we wended our way back to camp, arriving there about sunset, having been continuously under fire for nearly seven hours.

The losses on this day exceeded that of any since the siege began. Out of our small force engaged, 221 men were killed and wounded. It was computed that of the enemy more than 500 were killed, and probably twice that number wounded, the dead bodies lying thick together at every stage of our advance, but the wounded men in almost every instance were carried off by their comrades.

The camp of our regiment on the extreme left of the line having become a mere swamp and mud hole from the long-continued rain, and also being at too great a distance from the main body of the army, we were directed to change to a position close to the banks of the canal, near the General's headquarters, and on the left of the 8th Regiment. The move was made, I think, on July 11; and here we remained till the end of the siege.

At about this period, too, I was most agreeably surprised by a visit from an old school-fellow named C——d. He had entered the Bengal Civil Service a few years before, and, at the breaking out of the disturbances, was Assistant Collector at Goorgaon, seventeen miles from Delhi. On the death of their mother in Ireland, an only sister, a young girl of eighteen years of age, came out to India to take up her residence with him. C——d escorted his sister to Delhi on May 10, she having received an invitation to stay with the chaplain and his wife, who had quarters in the Palace. He returned to Goorgaon, little thinking he would never see her again.

The next morning, on the arrival of the insurgent cavalry from Meerut, and the subsequent mutiny of the native infantry regiments and artillery in the cantonments, the massacre of the Europeans in Delhi began.

I forbear entering into all the details of this dreadful butchery; suffice it to say that the chaplain, Mr. Jennings, his wife, Miss C——d, and nearly all the white people, both in the Palace and the city, were murdered. The editor of *The Delhi Gazette* and his family were tortured to death by having their throats cut with pieces of broken bottles, but there were conflicting accounts as to how the Jenningses and Miss C——d met their end. From what I gathered after the siege from some Delhi natives, it was reported that the ladies were stripped naked at the Palace, tied in that condition to the wheels of gun-carriages, dragged up the "Chandni Chauk," or silver street of Delhi, and there, in the presence of the King's sons, cut to pieces.

It was not till the following evening, May 12, that C——d heard of the Mutiny, and, fearing death from the populace of Goorgaon, who had also risen in revolt, he disguised himself as best he could and rode off into the country. After enduring great privations, and the danger of being taken by predatory bands, he at last reached Meerut, and thence accompanied the force to Delhi.

From what he hinted, I feel sure he had it on his mind that his sister, before being murdered, was outraged by the rebels. However this may be, my old school-fellow had become a changed being. All his passions were aroused to their fullest extent, and he thought of nothing but revenge. Armed with sword, revolver, and rifle, he had been present at almost every engagement with the mutineers since leaving Meerut. He was known to most of the regiments in camp, and would attach himself to one or the other on the occasion of a fight, dealing death with his rifle and giving no quarter. Caring nothing for his own life, so long as he succeeded in glutting his vengeance on the murderers of his sister, he exposed himself most recklessly throughout the siege, and never received a wound.

On the day of the final assault I met him in one of the streets after we had gained entrance into the city. He shook my hands, saying that he had put to death all he had come across, not excepting women and children, and from his excited manner and the appearance of his dress—which was covered with blood-stains—I quite believe he told me the truth. One would imagine he must have tired of slaughter during those six days' fighting in the city, but it was not so. I dined with him at the Palace the night Delhi was taken, when he told me he intended accompanying a small force the next morning to attack a village close by. All my remonstrances at this were of no avail; he vowed to me he would never stay his hand while he had an opportunity of wreaking his vengeance. Poor fellow! that was his last fight; advancing in front of the soldiers, he met his death from a bullet in the heart when assaulting the village.

There were other officers of the army in camp who had lost wives and relations at Delhi and Meerut, and who behaved in the same manner as C——d. One in particular, whose wife I had known well, was an object of pity to the whole camp. She was the first woman who was murdered during the outrage at Meerut, and her death took place under circumstances of such shocking barbarity that they cannot be recorded in these pages.

Truly these were fearful times, when Christian men and gallant soldiers, maddened by the foul murder of those nearest and dearest to them, steeled their hearts to pity and swore vengeance against the murderers. And much the same feelings, though not to such an extent, pervaded the breasts of all who were engaged in the suppression of the Mutiny. Every soldier fighting in our ranks knew that a day of reckoning would come for the atrocities which had been committed, and with unrelenting spirit dedicated himself to the accomplishment of that purpose. Moreover, it was on our part a fight for existence, a war of extermination, in which no prisoners were taken and no mercy shown—in short, one of the most cruel and vindictive wars that the world has seen. From July 10 to 14 there was comparative quiet in the camp; the cannonade continued on each side, but no sorties were made by the enemy.

July 12.—On the morning of the 12th I was detailed for picket duty at the Sabzi Mandi Gardens, to the right front of Hindoo Rao's house, the picket consisting of 100 men under the command of a Captain. Since the opening of the siege this had been the scene of many sanguinary encounters with the enemy, who put forth all their strength in endeavours to drive in the picket, and so turn our right flank at Hindoo Rao's house.

The view at first was almost completely closed in; but by the end of July the unremitting labours of the Engineers had cleared away the trees, walls, and buildings in front of the picket for some distance, and the earth-works connecting it with the ridge at Hindoo Rao's house were also completed.

I can remember no event of interest as occurring on July 12. Few shots were fired at us, and on being relieved the next morning we returned to camp, wondering at the unusual inactivity of the enemy.

July 14.—They were, however, only preparing for another sortie on a grand scale, and on the morning of the 14th the bugles again sounded the "alarm" and the "assembly." The insurgents poured out of the Kabul and Lahore Gates in great numbers, making, as usual, for the Sabzi Mandi Gardens and the right of the ridge. They kept up a constant fire of musketry and field-artillery; and though our batteries swept their masses with shell and round-shot, they still continued the attack, pressing close to the pickets and Hindoo Rao's house.

Shortly after midday a column of some 1,500 men was assembled to dislodge and drive them back to the city. We took the road as on the 9th, and soon became engaged with the enemy in the Sabzi Mandi Gardens. The struggle was long and fierce, a perpetual interchange of musketry and artillery, our losses, especially in officers, being very severe. The city batteries also sent grape and canister amongst us from their large guns and howitzers, inflicting mortal wounds, even at the great distance of 1,100 yards.

When driving the rebels before us past the suburb of Kishenganj, Lieutenant Gabbett and I, in the confusion of the rush, became separated from the few men of our regiment who were engaged on that day, and found ourselves—we being the only officers present—with about fifty soldiers of different corps. For more than half an hour we were completely isolated from the main body, and were occupied in several little fights on our own account. Advancing, we scarcely knew where, and in our excitement fully engaged in chasing the foe, we all at once came most unexpectedly on to a broad road, with open ground on each side. There, to our front, and scarcely 500 yards distant, we saw a gate with embattled towers, the high walls of the city, and a bastion. We were soon descried by the enemy, who depressed their guns and fired at us with grape, fortunately without hitting any of our party. We were in a complete dilemma, under fire of the batteries, cut off from our force, and liable at any moment to be surrounded; so, deeming discretion the better part of valour, we turned about and ran with all speed to the rear, coming upon a troop of Horse Artillery, which was halted amongst some gardens.

Soon the main body of our force returned from the pursuit of the rebels, whom they had driven to within 600 yards of the city wall; and joining our own detachment, who had given us up as lost, we returned to camp about sundown.

Again we had to lament the loss of many fine officers and soldiers. Nearly 200 men had been killed and wounded—a sad diminution of our little army, which, had it long continued, would have entirely decimated the Delhi Field Force. The enemy, however, had suffered most severely, their loss amounting to quite 1,000 men; and the next morning they were seen for hours carting the dead bodies into the city. Unusual bravery was shown by the rebels on this day: they stood fairly in the open, and also attacked the pickets with great pertinacity, assaulting one called the "Sammy House" for hours, and leaving eighty dead bodies in its front, all killed by the infantry of the Guides, who most gallantly held the picket against overwhelming numbers.

Cholera all this time raged in the force, and carried off its victims daily, my own regiment and the 8th being the principal sufferers. It was melancholy to enter the hospital, to see the agony and hear the groans of the men, many of them with their dying breath lamenting the hard fate which had stretched them on a sick-bed and prevented them from doing their duty in the ranks against the enemy. Fever and ague, too, were very prevalent, and hospital gangrene broke out, which attained such virulence that many wounded died from its effects; while of amputations, I believe not one recovered during the whole siege.

We were also in the midst of the Indian monsoon, the most unhealthy season of the year, when rain descended in torrents almost every day, a hot, muggy atmosphere increasing the sickness and adding to the eternal plague of flies, a plague the most nauseating it has ever been my lot to experience. When off duty, it was the custom of some of the officers to pass the time fishing in the canal at our rear. Here, seated on camp-stools brought out by our servants, we amused ourselves for hours, holding lotteries as to who would catch the first fish, the prize being a bottle of beer. To see us on these occasions, full of merriment, one would scarcely have realized the fact that the men employed in this peaceful occupation were part of an army engaged in almost continual warfare, and fighting for very existence. Laughter and jokes filled the air, and chaff reigned supreme; while ever and anon we were rudely recalled to a sense of the dangers around us by the report of a shell bursting over the ridge, or the presence of an orderly, who summoned one of the party to proceed on picket or on some perilous duty at the front.

With regard to provisions, we were plentifully supplied with regular meals, a sufficiency of good food and drinkables; our lot in this respect was far more enjoyable than that of the usual run of campaigners. A large flock of fat sheep accompanied us on the march down from Ferozepore; and I shall never forget the agony of mind of one of our gourmands when one day it was reported that the sheep had all been carried off by the enemy when grazing in the rear of the canal. I had also purchased 100 dozen of ale at Umballah for the use of the mess, and this being noised abroad in the camp, we were visited by several thirsty souls from other regiments, who, less fortunate than ourselves, had neglected furnishing themselves with this tempting beverage. It was a pleasure to us to minister to their wants, though I need hardly say that the stock lasted but a short time, from the numerous calls made on it.

July 17.—General Reed, who had taken command of the army on the death of Sir Henry Barnard, resigned his position on July 17 in consequence of sickness and the infirmities of old age. He was succeeded by General Wilson, of the Artillery, an officer who had already greatly distinguished himself, and under whom the siege was eventually brought to a successful conclusion.

July 18.—For three days after the last sortie the enemy were singularly quiet, quarrelling amongst themselves, as it was reported, and disputing as to what portion of their army was to lead the next sortie. However, on July 18, they again made another attempt upon the Sabzi Mandi and the ridge at Hindoo Rao's.

The force sent to dislodge them was under command of Colonel Jones, of the 60th Rifles, who made his arrangements with singular judgment and tact, and insisted on a regular formation being kept by the troops, instead of the desultory style of action in vogue during previous sorties. There was, however, some very hard fighting in the gardens and *serais*, where we were received by a storm of bullets; but the men being persuaded to keep well under cover, the losses were not very serious, the casualties amounting in all to about ninety officers and men.[2] The enemy, as usual, suffered severely, more especially from the fire of our field-guns, which mowed them down when collected in groups of two and three hundred together.

I was amused on this day, as well as on previous sorties, by seeing the eagerness with which the soldiers, European, Sikh, and Goorkha, rifled the bodies of the slain sepoys. These last had plundered the city inhabitants of all

---

2: Lieutenant Pattoun was wounded in the ankle on this occasion, and a sergeant of the 61st was shot through the head.

they could find in money and jewels, and having no place of safety (from the anarchy which prevailed in Delhi) in which to deposit their loot, they one and all invariably carried their treasure about with them, concealed in the *kammerbund* folds of muslin or linen rolled round the waist. On the fall of a mutineer, a rush would be made by the men to secure the coveted loot, a race taking place sometimes between a European and one of our native soldiers as to who should first reach the body. The *kammerbund* was quickly torn off and the money snatched up, a wrangle often ensuing among the men as to the division of the booty. In this manner many soldiers succeeded, to my knowledge, in securing large sums of money; one in particular, a Grenadier of my regiment, after killing a sepoy, rifled the body, and, returning in great glee to where I was standing, showed me twenty gold mohurs, worth £32 sterling. It was a most reprehensible practice, but almost impossible entirely to prevent, for in the loose order of fighting which generally prevailed, the men did not break from their ranks to accomplish their purpose, but often, in isolated groups of two and three, were separated at times a short distance from the rest of the combatants.

The General, we heard, was loud in his praise of the manner in which Colonel Jones conducted the operations on this day; after the action also, he withdrew his men in perfect order, allowing no straggling—a great contrast to our former usual style when returning to camp after the repulse of a sortie.

This was the last action of any consequence fought in the open at the Sabzi Mandi Gardens. The ground in front of the picket was soon after cleared, and during future attacks our men remained behind the breastworks and entrenchments which had been thrown up, and by a steady fire soon drove back any rebels who were foolhardy enough to come within range.

It speaks well for the prowess of the mutineers, and proves that we had no contemptible foe to deal with, that so many sorties and attacks were made by them during the siege. They amounted in all to thirty-six—all of these being regularly organized actions and assaults—besides innumerable others on isolated pickets and advanced posts. They seldom came to close quarters with our men, and then only when surprised; but nothing could exceed their persistent courage in fighting almost every day, and, though beaten on every occasion with frightful loss, returning over and over again to renew the combat.

July 19.—The succeeding days from July 19 to 23 were days of quiet, with the exception of the usual artillery duel. We took our turn at picket duty with the other regiments, one day at the Metcalfe house and stables, and on another at the Sabzi Mandi.

July 23.—On the morning of the 23rd the insurgents, for the first time since the previous month, made a sortie on our left, emerging from the Kashmir Gate with infantry and field-guns. With the latter they occupied Ludlow Castle, a ruined house midway between the Flagstaff Tower and the Kashmir Gate. Then they opened fire on the left of the ridge, and moving about continually amongst the trees and buildings, were well sheltered from our batteries, which were unable to make good practice. The rebels also showed at the Metcalfe picket, attacking at the same time with their infantry; and becoming emboldened by receiving no opposition from us, the greater part of their force advanced nearer and nearer to the ridge, till they were seen distinctly from the Mosque battery.

To punish their temerity, a force of all arms was sent out from camp under Brigadier Showers, with the intention of attacking their right flank. We moved up a deep gorge, and coming on them by surprise, forced them to remove their guns, which quickly limbered up and made for the city.

There was a great deal of skirmishing in the gardens and ruined houses before the infantry followed the example of their comrades; but the fight was not nearly so severe as during the sorties on the right, nor did the enemy suffer any very great loss. On our side, we had in all fifty officers and men killed and wounded.[3]

Again for some days the enemy made no movement, and the weather also holding up for a time, some sport was inaugurated in the camp. The men might be seen amusing themselves at various games, while the officers actually got up an impromptu horse-race.

This, however, was not to last long, and on July 31 we were again on the alert from the report that several thousands of rebels, with thirteen guns and mortars, were making for the open country to the right rear of our camp.

A force under Major Coke was sent out to watch their movements, and also to convoy a large store of treasure and ammunition coming down to us from the Punjab. The convoy arrived safe on the morning of August 1, and the rain falling heavily on that day, making the ground impassable for guns, the insurgent force, which had moved to our rear, broke up their camp and retired towards Delhi.

The 1st of August was the anniversary of a great Mohammedan festival called the *Bakra Id*, and for some time there had been rumours of a grand sortie in honour of the event.

Morning and afternoon passed, and we began to think the enemy had given up their purpose, when about sunset firing began at the right pickets. The mutineers returning from our rear had met an equal number, which had sallied from the city, at the suburb of Kishenganj, and the forces, joining together, moved forward and attacked the whole

---

3: Colonel Seton, 35th Native Infantry, was wounded in the stomach in this affair.

right of the ridge and the pickets in that quarter.

Loudly the bugles sounded the alarm all over the camp, and in a very short time every available man was mustered, and the troops were hurried forward to reinforce the breast-works at Hindoo Rao's house and on each side.

There had been only one actual night-attack since the beginning of the siege, and that took place to the rear; it therefore naturally occurred to the officers in command that this assault by the enemy with such vast numbers would require all our efforts to prevent being turned, thus imperilling the safety of the camp.

The action had commenced in earnest when we arrived on the ridge, and the brave defenders of Hindoo Rao's house were holding their own against enormous odds. Masses of infantry with field-guns swarmed in our front, yelling and shouting like demons while keeping up a steady fire.

Darkness came on—a lovely night, calm and clear without a cloud in the sky. The batteries on both sides kept up a terrific cannonade; and our men, effectually concealed behind the earth-works, poured incessant volleys of mus-ketry into the enemy. The roar and din exceeded anything I had ever heard before, and formed one continuous roll, while all around the air was illumined by a thousand bright flashes of fire, exposing to our view the movements of the rebels. They had also thrown up breastworks at no great distance to our front, from behind which they sallied at in-tervals, returning, however, quickly under cover when our fire became too hot for them. And in this manner, without a moment's intermission, the combat continued all night long, with no advantage to the assailants, and with few cas-ualties on our side.[4]

August 2.—Morning broke without any cessation in the

4: One man of the 61st Regiment was killed by a round-shot, which in its course also knocked over some sandbags which sent Lieutenant Hutton fly-ing about seven feet.

firing; and it was not till ten o'clock that the rebels, seeing how futile were all efforts, began to retire. Some few still kept up the firing; but at 2 p. m. all was quiet, and our sadly harassed soldiers were enabled to obtain some rest after seventeen hours' fighting. Nothing could have surpassed the steadiness of the men and the cool manner in which they met the attacks of the enemy, remaining well under cover, and only showing themselves when the rebels came close up. Our casualties during those long hours only amounted to fifty killed and wounded, thus proving the judgment of the General in ordering the men to remain behind the earthworks, and not to advance in pursuit unless absolutely necessary. Two hundred dead bodies were counted in front of the entrenchments, and doubtless during the darkness many more were carried off by the enemy.

After the severe lesson they had received the rebels remained inactive for some days, very few shots even being fired from the walls. We learnt that the late grand attack had been made by the Neemuch and part of the Gwalior and Kotah insurgents who had mutinied at those places not long before. This accounted for the stubbornness of the assault, it being the custom, when reinforcements arrived, to send them out at once to try their mettle with the besiegers.

The fruits of General Wilson's accession to the command of the army, and the stringent orders issued by him for the maintenance of order and discipline both in camp and on picket became more and more apparent every day. All duties were now regulated and carried out with the utmost precision; each regiment knew its allotted place in case of a sortie, and the officers on picket had to furnish reports during their term of duty, thereby making them more attentive to the discipline and care of their men. In the matter of uniform, also, a great and desirable change was made. Many corps had become quite regardless of appearance, entirely discarding all pretensions to uniformity, and adopting the most nondescript dress. One in particular, a most gallant regiment of Europeans which had served almost from the beginning of the siege, was known by the sobriquet of the "Dirty Shirts," from their habit of fighting in their shirts with sleeves turned up, without jacket or coat, and their nether extremities clad in soiled blue dungaree trousers.

The army in general wore a cotton dress, dyed with khaki rang, or dust colour, which at a distance could with difficulty be seen, and was far preferable to white or to the scarlet of the British uniform. The enemy, on the contrary, appeared entirely in white, having soon discarded the dress of their former masters; and it was a pretty sight to see them turning out of the gates on the occasion of a sortie, their arms glittering, pennons flying, and their whole appearance presenting a gay contrast to the dull, dingy dress of their foes.

August 5.—On August 5 an attempt was made by our Engineers to blow up the bridge of boats across the Jumna, and some of us went to the top of the Flagstaff Tower to see the result.

Two rafts filled with barrels of powder and with a slow match in each were sent down the river, starting from a point nearly a mile up the stream. We saw them descending, carried down slowly by the flood, one blowing up half a mile from the bridge. The other continued its course, and was descried by some mutineers on the opposite bank, who sent off men to the raft on *massaks* (inflated sheep-skins). It was a perilous deed for the men, but without any delay they made their way to the raft, put out the fuse, and towed the engine of destruction to shore. A most ignominious failure, and the attempt was never repeated, the bridge remaining intact to the last.

August 6.—At 7 a.m. on August 6 the alarm again

sounded, and we remained accoutred in camp for some hours, but were not called to the front on that day. A large party of the enemy's cavalry—more, it must be supposed, in a spirit of bravado than anything else—charged up the road towards the Flagstaff Tower, waving their swords and shouting, "*Din! din!*" A battery was brought to bear on them, and this, with a volley or two of musketry, soon sent them to the right about, galloping off and disappearing amongst the trees, after leaving some dead on the ground.

The enemy's infantry also harassed the pickets on the right flank, causing some casualties, and their artillery fire was kept up all day, the guns in the new Kishenganj battery almost enfilading the right of our position. No efforts on our part could silence the fire from this place, and it remained intact, a constant source of annoyance, to the end of the siege.

The numerous cavalry of the enemy might have caused us a vast amount of trouble had they been properly led, or behaved even as well as the infantry and artillery. But there seemed to be little dash or spirit amongst them, and though they made a brave show, emerging from the gates in company with the rest of their forces, waving swords and brandishing spears, they took care to keep at a respectful distance from our fire, their only exploit, as far as I can remember, being that on July 9, when 100 horsemen charged into the rear of our camp.

From the 8th to the 11th there were constant attacks on all the pickets, and the artillery fire on both sides was almost unceasing. The enemy brought out some guns by the Kashmir Gate and shelled the Metcalfe pickets, their skirmishers advancing close to our defences with shouts, and harassing the men day and night, though with small loss on our side. They also made the approach to the pickets for relief so perilous that at early morn of the 12th a large force, under Brigadier Showers, was detailed to drive the rebels into the city. My regiment furnished twenty men, under an officer,[5] on this occasion.

August 12.—We attacked them at dawn, taking them completely by surprise, and capturing all their guns, four in number. The 1st Fusiliers and Coke's Rifles behaved most gallantly, and bore the brunt of the fight, losing half the number of those killed and wounded—namely, 110. The enemy's casualties amounted to upwards of 300, and they left many wounded on the ground, who were shot and bayoneted without mercy. This signal chastisement had the effect of cowing them for a time, and the pickets on the left were unmolested for the future, save by occasional shots from the city batteries.

August 14.—August 14 was quiet, the enemy giving us a respite and scarcely firing a gun, though they must have known of the welcome reinforcements we had received that morning. These consisted of nearly 3,000 men, of which number more than 1,100 were Europeans.

This force, under command of General Nicholson, comprised the 52nd Regiment, our left wing from Ferozepore, some Mooltani Horse, 1,200 Sikhs and Punjabees, and a battery of European artillery. The reinforcements brought up the Delhi Field Force to more than 8,000 effectives, while of sick and wounded we had the frightful number of nearly 2,000 in camp, many more having been sent away to Umballah.

But what added most to our strength was the presence amongst us of the hero John Nicholson, he who has been since designated as the "foremost man in India." Young in years, he had already done good service in the Punjab wars, and was noted not only for his striking military talent, but also for the aptitude he displayed in bringing into

---

5: Lieutenant Yonge.

subjection and ruling with a firm hand the lawless tribes on our North-West Frontier. Many stories are told of his prowess and skill, and he ingratiated himself so strongly amongst a certain race that he received his apotheosis at their hands, and years afterwards was, and perhaps to this day is, worshipped by these rude mountaineers under the title of "Nikul Seyn." Spare in form, but of great stature, his whole appearance and mien stamped him as a "king of men." Calm and self-confident, full of resource and daring, no difficulties could daunt him; he was a born soldier, the idol of the men, the pride of the whole army. His indomitable spirit seemed at once to infuse fresh vigour into the force, and from the time of his arrival to the day of the assault Nicholson's name was in everyone's mouth, and each soldier knew that vigorous measures would be taken to insure ultimate success.

We were freed from attack for some days, and the only event of importance was a raid made by the enemy's horsemen in the direction of Rohtak. They were followed by that great irregular leader Hodson, who succeeded, with small loss, in cutting up some thirty of their number, his own newly-raised regiment and the Guide Cavalry behaving admirably.

August 19.—On August 19 a noteworthy incident occurred at the Sabzi Mandi picket. A woman dressed in the native costume, and attended by an Afghan, walked up to the sentries at that post, and on approaching the men, threw herself on her knees, thanking God in English that she was under the protection of British soldiers. The honest fellows were greatly taken aback, and wondered who this could be dressed in native costume, speaking to them in their own language. She was brought before the officer commanding the picket, when it transpired that she was a Eurasian named Seeson, the wife of a European road sergeant. During the outbreak on May 11 at Delhi her children had been slain before her eyes and she herself badly wounded, escaping, however, from the murderers in a most providential manner, and finding shelter in the house of a friendly native, who had succoured her ever since. By the aid of the Afghan, and disguised as an *ayah*, or nurse, she had passed through the gates of the city that morning, eventually finding her way to the picket. We had one lady in camp, the wife of an officer of native infantry, and to her kindly charge the poor creature was consigned, living to the end of the siege in Mrs. Tytler's tent, and being an object of curiosity as well as of pity to the whole force.

The enemy, lately, had caused great annoyance by firing at the ridge 32-pound rockets, a large store of which they had found in the magazine, and as they were unused to discharging these dangerous missiles, the rockets at first, by their rebound, inflicted more damage on the rebels than on us; but, gaining experience through long practice, they every evening and during part of the night fired them at the ridge, one or two falling right amongst the tents in camp.[6]

A battery also was erected about this time on the opposite bank of the Jumna, at a distance of some 2,000 yards from the Metcalfe pickets, and this was served so well that not only were the outposts in considerable danger from the fire, but the camp of one of our native regiments on the extreme left, and below the Flagstaff Tower, was shifted in consequence of the enemy's shells falling in their midst.

It will thus be seen that the rebels put forth their whole strength and used every means at their disposal to harass and annoy us. Like a swarm of hornets, they attacked us in every direction, first in one quarter and then in another; but no effort of theirs affected in the smallest degree the

---

6: On August 7 they blew up one of their own powder factories, and with it a number of workmen.

bulldog grip of the British army on the rebellious city. Reports were rife that the King had sent to propose terms to the General, and that the answer was a cannonade directed on the walls by all our batteries; also that their ammunition was falling short; but these, with other silly rumours, were merely the gossip of the camp, and were not credited by the bulk of the army.

August 24.—Again, a very large body of mutineers, numbering, it was said, 9,000 men, with thirteen guns, left the city on August 24. They were seen from the ridge for hours trooping out of the Lahore and Ajmir Gates, and proceeding far to our right rear. Their intention, no doubt, was to cut off the large siege-train and munitions of war on their way down to us from the arsenal at Ferozepore.

August 25.—A force was at once detailed, under command of the gallant Nicholson, to intercept the enemy and, if possible, to bring them to battle. Long before daylight on the morning of August 25 we paraded, cavalry, infantry, and three batteries of Horse Artillery, or eighteen guns, numbering in all nearly 2,500 men.

At six o'clock the march began, and leaving the Grand Trunk road a short distance from the rear of our camp, we made across country to a town named Nanglooi, distant six miles. The men were in high spirits notwithstanding the difficulties we had to encounter in traversing a route well-nigh impassable from the recent rains, and ankle-deep in mud. Two broad swamps also had to be crossed, the soldiers wading waist-high in the water, and carrying their ammunition-pouches on their heads. Three hours and more were passed before we arrived at the village, and here information reached the General that the enemy were posted twelve miles distant, at a place named Najafgarh.

The march was at once resumed, and, floundering in the mud, the artillery horses especially with great labour dragging the guns through the morass which extended nearly all the way, we arrived at about four o'clock on the banks of a canal in full view of the enemy's position.

This had been chosen with great judgment, and presented a formidable appearance, stretching about a mile and a half from the canal bridge on the extreme right to a large serai on the left in the town of Najafgarh. Nine guns were posted between the bridge and the *serai*, with four more in the latter building, all protected by entrenchments with parapets and embrasures.

The troops crossed the canal by a ford, and formed up in line of battle on the opposite side, facing the town of Najafgarh, and about 900 yards from the *serai*, the infantry in two lines, ourselves and the 1st Bengal Fusiliers in front, with artillery and cavalry on each flank.

When we were halted, Nicholson came to the front and, addressing the regiments of European infantry, spoke a few soul-stirring words, calling on us to reserve our fire till close to the enemy's batteries, and then to charge with fixed bayonets. He was answered with a cheer, and the lines advanced across the plain steady and unbroken, as though on parade.

The enemy had opened fire, and were answered by our guns, the infantry marching with sloped arms at the quick step till within 100 yards, when we delivered a volley. Then the war-cry of the British soldiers was heard, and the two regiments came to the charge, and ran at the double towards the serai.

Lieutenant Gabbett of my regiment was the first man to reach the entrenchment, and, passing through an embrasure, received a bayonet thrust in the left breast, which stretched him on the ground. The men followed, clearing everything before them, capturing the four guns in the serai, bayoneting the rebels and firing at those who had taken to flight at our approach. Then, changing front, the whole force swept along the entrenchment to the bridge, making a clean sweep of the enemy, who turned and fled, leaving the remaining nine guns in our hands.

Our Horse Artillery, under Major Tombs—never better served than in this action—mowed down the fugitives in hundreds, and continued following and firing on them till darkness set in. The cavalry also—a squadron of the gallant 9th Lancers, with the Guides and Punjabees—did their share of work, while the European infantry were nobly supported by the corps of Punjab Rifles, who cleared the town of the sepoys.

The battle had lasted a very short time, and after dark we bivouacked on the wet ground in the pouring rain, completely exhausted from our long march and subsequent fighting, and faint from want of food, none of which passed our lips for more than sixteen hours.

Still, the day's work was not over. A village to the rear was found to be occupied by the enemy, and the Punjab Rifles were ordered to take it. They met with a most obstinate resistance, their young commander, Lumsden, being killed. The General then sent part of my regiment to dislodge the rebels, but we met with only partial success, and had one officer, named Elkington, mortally wounded, the enemy evacuating the place during the night.

We passed the night of the 25th in the greatest discomfort. Hungry and wet through, we lay on the ground, snatching sleep at intervals. Poor Gabbett died of internal haemorrhage soon after he received his wound, and his death deprived the regiment of one of its best and bravest officers, and me of a true friend. He had shared my tent on the march down and during the whole campaign, a cheery, good-hearted fellow, and one who had earned the respect of officers and the love of his men. The General was particularly struck with his bravery, and with feeling heart wrote a letter to Gabbett's mother, saying he would have recommended her son for the Victoria Cross had he survived the action.

Young Elkington also received his death-wound at the night-attack on the village. He was quite a stripling, being only eighteen years old, and had joined the regiment but a few months before. His was one of those strange cases of a presentiment of death, many of which have been well authenticated in our army. On looking over his effects, it was found that he had written letters to his nearest relations on the night before marching to Najafgarh; and he had also carefully made up small parcels of his valuables and trinkets, with directions on them to whom they were to be delivered in case of his being killed next day. It was noticed, too, that he was unusually quiet and reserved, never speaking a word to anyone on the march, though when the action began he behaved like a gallant soldier, giving up his young life in the service of his country.

August 26.—On the morning of August 26 we marched back to camp, arriving there before sundown, and were played in by the bands of the two regiments, while many soldiers, native as well as European, lined the road and gave us a hearty cheer.

Our casualties at the action of Najafgarh amounted to twenty-five officers and men killed and seventy wounded. The enemy left great numbers of dead in the entrenchments and on the plain, their loss being computed at 500 killed and wounded; but this, I fancy, is much below the mark, for our artillery fire was very destructive, and the cavalry committed great havoc amongst the host of fugitives. The battle of the 25th was the most brilliant and decisive since that of Badli-ki-Serai on June 8. All the guns, thirteen in number, were captured, and the enemy's camp, ammunition, stores, camels and bullocks were taken. Would that we had met the insurgents oftener in the open in this manner! But the rascals were too wary, and had too great a dread of our troops to face them in a pitched encounter.

During the absence of Nicholson's small force the enemy had attacked all the pickets, and kept up a heavy cannonade from the walls, causing us a loss of thirty-five men. It was their impression that the camp had been left almost bare and defenceless by the withdrawal of so large a force; but they were quickly undeceived, and were met at each point of assault by a galling fire from our men.

For many nights after August 26 our right pickets were constantly harassed by the rebels, who also shelled Hindoo Rao's house from the city and Kishenganj batteries. Our sappers, too, found it not only difficult, but dangerous, to work in the advanced trenches below the ridge, being always met by a murderous musketry from the enemy's sharpshooters, who fired down behind breastworks. It was resolved, therefore, on August 30, to drive them out from their cover, and on two or more occasions this was performed by the Goorkhas and the 60th Rifles, who, as usual, fighting together and supporting each other, took the breastworks in gallant style. Our Engineers were then enabled to continue their operations in the trenches preparatory to making approaches towards the city walls, and constructing the batteries for the siege-train, now daily expected.

The Flagstaff Tower, as I have already mentioned in a former part of my narrative, was the chief rendezvous of officers when not on duty. About this time I went to the top of the tower in company with one of my regiment, when an amusing incident occurred.

We were watching the batteries playing on each side, when a tall Afghan, armed to the teeth, appeared at the top of the steps, and was about to set foot on the enclosed space under the flagstaff. A sentry was always stationed there, and on this occasion it happened to be a sturdy little Goorkha, one of the Kumaon battalion. On the approach of the Afghan he immediately came to the charge, and warned him that none but European officers were allowed on the top of the tower. The Afghan laughed, and then, looking with contempt at the diminutive sentry, a dwarf in comparison with himself, he attempted to push aside the bayonet. Losing all patience, the Goorkha at this threw down his musket, and drawing his kukri, the favourite weapon of his race, he rushed at the Afghan with up-lifted blade. This was too much for our valiant hero, who quickly turned tail, and disappeared down the circular staircase, the Goorkha following him at a short distance. On his return he picked up the musket, and seeing us laughing, the frown on his face turned into the most ludicrous expression of good-humour I had ever seen, and he burst out into a fit of laughter which lasted some minutes. He told us that he and the other Goorkhas of his regiment thought nothing of the bravery of the Afghan soldiers, some 100 of whom were on our side at Delhi; and he spoke truly.

These men, all cavalry, superbly mounted, dressed in chain armour, and carrying arms of every description, had been sent down ostensibly as a reinforcement to us by their Ameer, Dost Mohammed Khan of Kabul, but really as spies to watch our movements, and report the state of affairs to their chief. They made a great display about the camp, but I never heard of their meeting the enemy in action during their stay before Delhi.

The last two days of August we had several men killed and wounded in the force, and one of our officers, who shared my tent after poor Gabbett's death, received a severe contusion from the bursting of a shell.

Nearly three months had now elapsed since the Siege of Delhi began. We were, to all appearance, no nearer to the desired end, and had scarcely gained one foot of ground nearer to the walls of the city. Moreover, there was alarm in the Punjab owing to a reported disaffection among the Sikh population, who, it is said, were beginning openly to assert that the British army was unable to take Delhi.

To check this feeling, the Chief Commissioner had urged General Wilson to lose no time in making preparations for the assault of the city; and thus our expectations beat high at the near approach of the powerful siege-train on its way down from Ferozepore, though we knew there were still before us trials and dangers to which our former experiences would be as nothing.

The weather had now somewhat cleared, but the heat was overpowering, averaging 98° in the shade of my tent every day. Cholera, too, raged as before, the principal sufferers being ourselves, and the 8th and 52nd Regiments. To cheer the soldiers, the bands played in camp of an evening, while some officers and men engaged in sport of various kinds; but the angel of Death was hovering over my poor regiment, and few of us had the heart to join in pastime while our comrades lay stricken and dying of disease in hospital.

September 1.—A portion of my corps was on duty at the Metcalfe stable picket on September 1, when a lamentable loss was experienced, unparalleled in the annals of the siege. The enemy's battery across the river had never ceased shelling these pickets, though up to this day it had not caused much damage to the defenders.

Shortly after sunrise the men were assembled outside, receiving their grog, which was served out to them every morning at an early hour. Some 100 men and officers, beside Sikhs and native attendants, were grouped around, when a loud hissing sound was heard, and a shrapnel shell, fired from the enemy's battery at the long range of 2,000 yards, exploded a few feet in front. The bullets scattered around, and the scene which followed it is almost impossible for me to depict. Many threw themselves flat on the ground, falling one on top of the other, while groans and cries were heard. One soldier fell mortally wounded by my side, and on looking around to count up our losses, we found that two of my regiment had been killed outright, besides six others severely wounded. Two Sikhs and a *bhisti*, or water-carrier, also met their death, and two doolie-bearers were wounded—thirteen men in all.

One very stout old officer was in the act of having his morning bath when the shell exploded, the *bhisti* standing at his side and pouring over him, when squatted on a tent-mallet, his massuck of water. He rolled over and over on the ground, presenting such a ludicrous appearance in his wet, nude state, and covered with earth, that, notwithstanding the awful surroundings of the scene, I and others could not forbear laughing. The shot had been quite a chance one, but it proved how deadly was the effect of a shrapnel shell exploding, as this had done, only a few feet in front of a large body of men.

September 2 and 3.—The batteries continued exchanging shots during September 2 and 3, but there were no attacks of any consequence on the pickets, and we had on those days only three men wounded on the right of our position.

On the morning of the 4th the long-looked-for siege-train reached camp. It consisted of twenty-four heavy guns and mortars, and a plentiful supply of ammunition and stores. Reinforcements also reached us, amounting to about 400 European infantry and the Belooch battalion, the last a most savage-looking lot of men, who, however, did good service, and fought well. Besides these, a party of Sikh horsemen, in the service of the Rajah of Jhind—a noble-looking man, who, with his retainers, had kept open our communications with the Punjab during the whole siege—joined the army, begging as a favour that they might join in the dangers of the coming assault on the city.

September 7.—September 7 also saw the arrival of Wilde's regiment of Punjabis, 700 strong, followed the same day by the Kashmir contingent of 2,200 men and four guns, sent to our assistance by the ruler of that country.

I was sitting in my tent with the bandmaster of my regiment, a German named Sauer, when we were saluted with the sound of distant music, the most discordant I have ever heard. The bandmaster jumped up from his seat, exclaiming: "*Mein Gott! vat is dat?* No regiment in camp can play such vile music," and closing his ears immediately, rushed out of the tent.

The Kashmir troops were marching into camp, accompanied by General Wilson and his staff, who had gone out to meet them, their bands playing some English air, drums beating, and colours flying. There was no fault to be found in the appearance of the soldiers, who were mostly Sikhs and hill men of good physique; but their ludicrous style of marching, the strange outlandish uniform of the men, and the shrill discord of their bands, created great amusement among the assembled Europeans, who had never seen such a travesty on soldiers before. They encamped on our right flank; but were not employed on active service till the day of assault, on September 14.

On the arrival of the siege-train, no time was lost in making approaches and parallels, and erecting batteries for the bombardment of Delhi. The trench-work had already been begun, and what with covering and working parties, both of European and native soldiers, and the usual picket duties, the greater part of the army was continually employed in this arduous work every night and a portion of each day. Nothing could surpass the zeal and willing aptitude of the men, who laboured unceasingly digging trenches and filling sand-bags, all the time, and more especially at night, exposed to a galling fire of musketry and shells.

The Engineers, under their able leaders, were unremitting in their duties; and the young officers of that corps covered themselves with glory both in these preliminary operations and at the actual assault.

No. 1 Battery, to our right front, consisting of ten heavy

guns and mortars, was traced, on the evening of September 7, about 700 yards from the Mori bastion. No. 2, to the left front, near Ludlow Castle, and only 600 yards from the walls, was completed on the 10th, and contained nineteen pieces of artillery.

No. 4, for ten heavy mortars, and near No. 2, at the Koodsia Bagh, was completed in front of the Kashmir bastion also on that day. And, lastly, No. 3, on the extreme left, with six guns at the short distance of 180 yards from the Water bastion, was unmasked behind the Custom-House, which was blown up after the completion of the battery.

Thus, in four days and nights, after incredible exertions on the part of the working parties, forty-five heavy guns and mortars were in position, strongly entrenched, and ready to silence the fire from the enemy's bastions and to make breaches in the walls for the assaulting columns.

The rebels during all this time plied the covering and working parties with shot and shell, bringing out field-guns, which enfiladed the Ludlow Castle and Koodsia Bagh batteries, and keeping up a sharp musketry fire from an advanced trench they had dug in front of the walls. At the two latter places, where the men of my regiment were employed, the fire was very galling at times, the guns from the distant Selimgarh Fort, Water, and Kashmir bastions all concentrating their shots at those batteries whilst in process of erection.

The nights, fortunately, were clear, and we had plenty of light to assist us in our work; the men were cheerful and active, never resting for a moment in their labours, and receiving in the Field Force orders the praise of the General in command.

We wondered how it was that the enemy allowed us to occupy the advanced positions at Ludlow Castle and the Koodsia Bagh without even so much as a struggle; but it was accounted for by the supposition that they imagined our attack would be made from the right of our position, where all the great conflicts had taken place. There they were in strength, and it was our weakest point; whereas, on the side near the Jumna, we were protected from being turned by having the river on our flank, better cover for operations, and, moreover, batteries to silence which were less powerful and more difficult of concentration than those which faced us on our right from the city walls and from the suburb of Kishenganj.

CHAPTER 4
Capture of the City

The actual Siege of Delhi may be said to have commenced on September 7, 1857. All reinforcements that could possibly arrive had reached us with the siege-train, and the effective force now available for operations before Delhi consisted of the following troops:

European	Artillery	580
	Cavalry	514
	Infantry	2,672
	TOTAL	3,766
Native	Artillery	770
	Cavalry	1,313
	Infantry	3,417
	Engineers Sappers Miners, etc.	722
	TOTAL	6,222
	GRAND TOTAL	9,988

To the above must be added the Kashmir contingent of 2,200 men, with four guns, and the cavalry of the Jhind Rajah, perhaps 400 more, making the full amount of troops employed at the siege 12,588.

The seven regiments of European infantry were sadly reduced in numbers, being mere skeletons, the strongest mustering 409 effective rank and file, and the weakest only

242. There were also nearly 3,000 men in hospital, Europeans and natives.

From the most reliable sources the enemy at this period numbered 40,000 men, all trained soldiers of the former regular army, besides undisciplined armed hordes of fanatics and rabble of the city and surrounding country—a formidable disproportion to our scanty force when it is recollected that they were protected by strong fortifications mounting upwards of fifty guns, with an unlimited supply of artillery and munitions of war, and that with their vast numbers they had ample opportunities of harassing our right flank and rear and cutting off communications up-country.

Nevertheless, political considerations demanded that we should take the offensive and deal such a blow as would convince the rebels, as well as those whose loyalty was wavering, that the British arms were irresistible. Moreover, there was no likelihood of our force being increased. So on September 7 General Wilson issued the following address to his troops:

> "The force assembled before Delhi has had much hardship to undergo since its arrival in this camp, all of which has been most cheerfully borne by officers and men. The time is now drawing near when the Major-General commanding the force trusts that its labours will be over, and it will be rewarded by the capture of the city for all its past exertions, and for a cheerful endurance of still greater fatigue and exposure. The troops will be required to aid and assist the Engineers in the erection of the batteries and trenches, and in daily exposure to the sun, as covering parties.
>
> "The artillery will have even harder work

than they yet have had, and which they have so well and cheerfully performed hitherto: this, however, will be for a short period only, and when ordered to the assault, the Major-General feels assured British pluck and determination will carry everything before them, and that the bloodthirsty and murderous mutineers against whom they are fighting will be driven headlong out of their stronghold, or be exterminated. But to enable them to do this, he warns the troops of the absolute necessity of their keeping together, and not straggling from their columns. By this can success only be secured.

"Major-General Wilson need hardly remind the troops of the cruel murders committed on their officers and comrades, as well as their wives and children, to move them in the deadly struggle. No quarter should be given to the mutineers; at the same time, for the sake of humanity and the honour of the country they belong to, he calls upon them to spare all women and children that may come in their way.

"It is so imperative, not only for their safety, but for the success of the assault, that men should not straggle from their column that the Major-General feels it his duty to direct all commanding officers to impress this strictly upon their men, and he is confident that after this warning the men's good sense and discipline will induce them to obey their officers and keep steady to their duty. It is to be explained to every regiment that indiscriminate plunder will not be allowed; that prize agents have been appointed, by whom all captured property will be collected and sold, to be divided, according to the rules and regulations on this head, fairly among all men engaged; and that any man found guilty of having concealed captured property will be made to restore it, and will forfeit all claims to the general prize; he will also be likely to be made over to the Provost-Marshal to be summarily dealt with.

"The Major-General calls upon the officers of the force to lend their zealous and efficient co-operation in the erection of the works of the siege now about to be commenced. He looks especially to the regimental officers of all grades to impress upon their men that to work in the trenches during a siege is as necessary and honourable as to fight in the ranks during a battle.

"He will hold all officers responsible for their utmost being done to carry out the directions of the Engineers, and he confidently trusts that all will exhibit a healthy and hearty spirit of emulation and zeal, from which he has no doubt that the happiest results will follow in the brilliant termination of all their labours."

September 7.—From the night of September 7 to the day of assault all the artillerymen in the force, European as well as native, were constantly employed in the batteries and trenches. Day and night officers and men worked with unflagging energy in the advanced batteries, with no relief and no cessation from their toil. Few in number, worn out by the excessive fatigues of a three months' campaign, and enervated by continuous work in the deadliest season of the year, these gallant European artillerymen earned during those last days of the siege, by their zeal and devotion, the heartfelt thanks of the whole army. The old Bengal Artillery have a splendid roll of services, extending for upwards of 100 years; still, in the annals of that distinguished regiment there is no brighter record than their achievements before Delhi in 1857. The corps has been merged into the Royal Artillery, but the ancient name still lives in the memory of those who were witnesses of their deeds, and their imperishable renown adds greater lustre to the proud motto, *Ubique*, borne by the regiment to which they are affiliated.

Many officers and men of the cavalry and infantry volunteered for service in the batteries when called on by the General. They acquitted themselves well, were of great use to the gunners in lightening the arduous duties, and were complimented in orders for the valuable aid they had afforded to their companions in arms.[1]

September 11.—The advanced batteries were all completed by the evening of September 11, when the actual bombardment of the city began. For three days and nights previous No. 1 Battery, on the extreme right, was severely pounded from the Mori bastion and Kishenganj, but when the guns got into full play the fire from the former grew gradually weaker and weaker, till it was completely overpowered. Nos. 2 and 4 Batteries, being nearer to the walls, suffered much from the enemy, and the losses were very severe both among the artillery and the covering and working bodies of infantry.

September 11.—At length, on September 11, the whole of our batteries opened fire simultaneously on the city bastions and walls. The Kashmir bastion was soon silenced, the ramparts and adjacent curtains knocked to fragments, and a large breach opened in the walls. On the extreme left, at the Custom-House, our battery, as before related, was only 180 yards from the city, and the crushing fire from this, when in full play, smashed to pieces the Water bastion, overturned the guns, and made a breach in the curtain so wide and practicable that it could be ascended with ease.

1: Lieutenant Boileau, 61st Regiment, served in the batteries till the end of the siege

Fifty guns and mortars were now pouring shot and shell without a moment's interval on the doomed city. The din and roar were deafening; day and night salvos of artillery were heard, roll following roll in endless succession, and striking terror in the hearts of those who knew and felt that the day of retribution was at hand.

Still, though their batteries on the bastions had been wellnigh silenced, the rebels stuck well to their field-guns in the open space before the walls; they sent a storm of rockets from one of the martello towers, and fired a stream of musketry from the ramparts and advanced trenches. Kishenganj, too, made its voice heard, harassing our right and sweeping the Sabzi Mandi and Hindoo Rao's with its incessant fire.

During the bombardment our casualties amounted to nearly 350 men, the enemy causing great loss at No. 2 Battery through the fire of a 3-pounder served from a hole broken in the curtain-wall. This gun was admirably directed, and could not be silenced notwithstanding all our efforts. One officer, looking over the parapet to see the effect of his fire, was struck by a shot from the "hole in the wall," his head being taken completely off, the mutilated trunk falling back amongst the men at the guns—a ghastly and terrible sight, which filled us who were present with horror.

During the whole of the bombardment portions of my regiment were on duty in the batteries and trenches, working at the repair of the parapets and embrasures occasionally damaged by the enemy's shot, and also taking their share of duty with the advanced and covering parties. These were harassing and dangerous services, involving great vigilance. We were almost always under fire from the enemy; but with the utmost cheerfulness, and even, I may say, good-humour, the whole of the infantry did all in their power to lighten the work of the overtasked artillerymen:

comrades we were, all striving for the accomplishment of one purpose—that of bringing swift and sure destruction on the rebels who had for so long a period successfully resisted our arms. So cool and collected had the men become that even in the midst of fire from the advanced trenches, and while keeping up on our side a brisk fusillade, the soldiers smoked their pipes, rude jokes were bandied from one to the other, and laughter was heard.

When off duty I and others took our station for hours on the ridge, and sometimes on the top of the Flagstaff Tower. Thence with eager eyes we watched the batteries cannonading the walls, and marked the effects of the round-shot on the ramparts and bastions. Few of the enemy could be seen; but every now and then some would show themselves, disappearing when a well-directed shot struck in too close proximity. Cavalry and infantry at times issued from the gates; but from their hurried movements it seemed evident that they were ill at ease, and after a short time they returned into the city.

At night the scene was, as may be supposed, grand in the extreme. The space below was lighted up by continuous flashes and bursts of flame, throwing a flood of light among the thick forest of trees and gardens, while shells would burst high over the city, illuminating the spires and domes, and bringing into prominence every object around. There was not only the roll of the heavy guns and mortars, but the sharp rattle of musketry, and the hiss of the huge rocket, as it cut through the air with its brilliant light, sounded in our ears.

September 12.—On the 12th the enemy made frequent sorties from the Lahore and Ajmir Gates with bodies of cavalry and foot, while a party of horsemen crossed the canal, and made for the right rear of the camp. The latter were seen by the Guides and some Punjabi cavalry, who, led by Probyn and Watson, advanced to meet the enemy. There was a short but sharp encounter at close quarters, in which thirty rebels were killed, the remainder flying at full speed towards the city. The sorties from the gates turned out comparatively harmless, and seemed meant only as demonstrations to draw out our troops from the cover of the advanced trenches. Seeing that the attempt was futile, and resulted only in loss to themselves, the enemy retreated in confusion, their flight being accelerated by shell and round-shot from No. 1 Battery, and musketry from our outlying posts.

A serious loss befell the army on this day in the death of Captain Robert Fagan, of the Bengal Artillery. This officer, whose heroism made his name conspicuous even among the many gallant spirits of the Delhi Field Force, was killed in No. 3 Advanced Battery, a post he had occupied since September 8, and which was more than any other exposed to the enemy's fire. He had served throughout the siege, and was beloved by his men, winning the hearts of all, not only by his undaunted behaviour and cool courage, but also by his kind-hearted and amiable disposition.

The approaching day of assault was now the subject of conversation among officers and men; for the end was at hand. On September 12 a council of war met in General Wilson's tent, at which all the superior officers of the army were present. All the arrangements for attack were perfected, and the position of every brigade and corps was fixed and decided, though the day and hour of assault was known to no one, not even to the General in command.

September 13.—There was no rest for us on the 13th, the last Sunday we were destined to pass before the walls of Delhi. The fire of our heavy cannon increased in violence every hour, and the silence of the enemy's batteries assured us of the efficacy of the bombardment, and the speedy approach of the time when our columns would move to the assault on the city.

That night, soon after darkness had set in, four officers of the Engineers proceeded to examine the two large breaches in the walls made by the batteries. It was a hazardous duty, exposing them to peril of their lives; but these brave young fellows executed their task in safety, and, unobserved by the enemy, few of whom seemed to be keeping watch on the ramparts, returned to report the perfect practicability of the breaches for escalade.

Then the General issued his orders for the final assault; and long before midnight each regiment in camp knew its allotted place in the coming attack on the city.

Five storming columns were formed, the position and details of each being as under:

> No. 1, under Brigadier General Nicholson, consisting of the 75th Regiment, 1st Bengal Fusiliers, and Punjab Infantry, to storm the breach at the Kashmir bastion—in all 1,000 men.

> No. 2 Column, under Brigadier W. Jones (H.M. 61st Regiment), consisting of H.M. 8th (the King's) Regiment, 2nd Europeans, 4th Sikhs—altogether 850 men to storm the breach near the Water bastion.

> No. 3, under Colonel Campbell, consisting of the 52nd Regiment, the Kumaon battalion of Goorkhas, and 1st Punjab Infantry—in all 950 men—to assault the Kashmir Gate after it should be blown in by the Engineers.

> No. 5, or the Reserve, under Brigadier Longfield (H.M. 8th Regiment), to follow No. 3 by that gate into the city, was composed of the 61st, the Belooch battalion, 4th Punjab Infantry, and the Jhind troops—altogether 1,300 men, with 200 of H.M. 60th Rifles—to cover the advance of Nicholson's column and to form a reserve.

The whole of the above-named columns were under the immediate command of General Nicholson, on whom devolved all arrangements for carrying out the assault on Delhi.

> No. 4 Column, under Major Reid, the officer in command at Hindoo Rao's house, was formed of part of the 60th Rifles, the Sirmoor battalion of Goorkhas, detachments from European regiments, and the Kashmir contingent. This column was to attack the fortified suburb of Kishenganj, and enter the city by the Lahore Gate, meeting Nos. 1 and 2 Columns at that place.

> The cavalry brigade, under Colonel Grant, composed of the 9th Lancers, part of the 6th Carabineers, with Sikh and Punjab cavalry and some Horse Artillery, took up their position on the right of No. 1 Advanced Battery, facing the Mori Gate, and within range of Kishenganj. Their object was to oppose any attempt to take the storming columns in flank, to watch the movements of the enemy, and to guard the camp from surprise.

To the convalescents and a small force of cavalry and artillery the protection of the camp was confided—a very insufficient guard when it is considered that the enemy might well, out of their vast numbers, have detached part of their horsemen and infantry to harass, if not imperil, its safety, and that of the many, sick and wounded. As will hereafter be seen, great danger resulted from the arrangements made in this respect; and had the enemy, after our unsuccessful attack on Kishenganj on the 14th, but shown a spirit of pluck and daring, it is not too much to affirm that the camp might have fallen into their hands, and our successes in the city have thereby been rendered almost nugatory.

The night of the 13th was passed by us in a cheerful mood, everyone hopeful and confident of what the morrow would bring forth. There was a character of determination among the officers and men, a cool, deliberate conviction that, under Providence, success would crown our arms, and that vengeance would be done on those who had forfeited their lives by the cruel massacre of our defenceless women and children.

Sleep visited the eyes of few in camp during the short hours of preparation for the assault. Fully equipped to turn out at a moment's notice, we lay down on our beds waiting for the signal to fall in. This came at about three o'clock on the morning of September 14—an auspicious day, it being the third anniversary of the Battle of the Alma.

September 14.—The troops fell in on their respective lines, and, assembling at the slope of the ridge, the four columns of attack marched in silence to the Flagstaff Tower. Thence, picking up the men on picket, who were all withdrawn from the outlying posts, the force moved by the road to the neighbourhood of Ludlow Castle, and close to No. 2 Advanced Battery. Our movements were entirely concealed from the enemy; the darkness which prevailed, and the ample cover from trees, gardens, and houses, masking the march of the columns, while the breaching batteries, which had kept up their fire all night long, still continued the bombardment; nor did they cease till the actual moment when the columns were set in motion and took their way to the city.

Just before sunrise all the dispositions were completed, the gallant Nicholson, under whose orders we were, moving from point to point to perfect his arrangements. Our artillery fire ceased as if by magic; and a stillness, which contrasted ominously with the former roar and din, must have convinced the rebels that something unusual was about to take place.

The 60th Rifles with a cheer advanced to the front, and opened out as skirmishers to the right and left of the Koodsia Bagh. Then followed Nos. 1 and 2 Columns, which, in compact order, issued from their cover, making for the two breaches to be assaulted.

I was with my regiment in No. 5 Column; and with breathless interest, each heart aflame with excitement, we watched our comrades marching to the attack. Presently the order for No. 3 Column to move forward was given, and at a short interval our own followed.

Meanwhile the enemy had descried our movements, and the ramparts and walls and also the top of the breaches were alive with men, who poured in a galling fire on our troops Soon they reached the outer edge of the moat, and amidst a perfect hailstorm of bullets, causing great havoc among our men, the scaling-ladders were let down. The ditch here, 20 feet deep and 25 feet broad, offered a serious obstacle to the quick advance of the assaulting columns; the men fell fast under the withering fire, and some delay ensued before the ladders could be properly adjusted. However, nothing daunted, the opposite side was scaled, and, mounting the escarp, the assailants, with shouts and cheers that could be heard above the din of battle, rushed up the two breaches.

Without waiting for the charge of the British bayonets, the greater part of the rebels deserted the walls and bastions and ran pell-mell into the city, followed by our men. Some few stood manfully and endeavoured to check the flight of the rest; but they were soon shot or bayoneted, and the two columns halted inside the walls.

Almost simultaneously with the entrance of our troops into the city, the Kashmir Gate was blown in, and No. 3 Column, followed by No. 5, advanced along the covered way and passed into the city. We had only been, met by desultory fire from the enemy, which caused few casualties, during our march to the gate; the men were in high spirits, and longed to come to close quarters.

The episode of the blowing in of the Kashmir Gate of Delhi is too well known to require description here;[2] suffice it to say that the deed was an act of heroism almost without a parallel in the annals of the British army. In broad daylight, a small band of heroes advanced to almost certain death; but with a determination and valour seldom heard of, after repeated attempts to lay the powder-bags and apply the match, and losing nearly all their number, killed and wounded, the gate was blown in, giving free passage to the assaulting columns.

All the troops were now assembled at the main guard, in an open space close to the Kashmir Gate, and here, as well as the firing from the enemy would permit, the force re-formed, under the orders of General Nicholson. Nos. 1 and 2 Columns united, and under command of that officer moved to their right, advancing along the walls in that direction and clearing everything in their way.

No. 3 Column now marched into the heart of the city, being guided by Sir Theophilus Metcalfe, and by a circuitous route made its way towards the Jama Musjid. Soon we lost sight of this force, and then our own work began.

Advancing from our first place at the main guard, No. 5 Column pushed forward to the College Gardens, marching through narrow streets and lanes, with high houses on each side. But how can I describe that terrible street-fighting, which lasted without intermission the whole day? From every window and door, from loopholes in the buildings, and from the tops of the houses, a storm of musketry saluted us on every side, while every now and then, when passing the corner of a street, field-guns, loaded with grape, discharged their contents into the column. Officers and men

2: Are not the names of the Engineers Home and Salkeld and of Bugler Hawthorne (H.M. 52nd Regiment) household words?

fell fast, but this only served to exasperate the remainder, who almost without a check reached the College, and, after some severe skirmishing, cleared the gardens and houses of the rebels, and bayoneted all who were found there.

Leaving a detachment to occupy this post, we passed through more streets and lanes, ever exposed to the same terrific fire, and after great trouble succeeded in taking possession of Colonel Skinner's house and a large building known as the palace of Ahmed Ali Khan.

It was now midday, and at the latter place we were joined by No. 3 Column, which, making its way to the Jama Musjid, met with such a strenuous resistance that, after losing many men, and being without powder with which to blow up the gates of the mosque, it was forced to retire. The streets, we heard, were alive with men on their line of route, and the column had been exposed to incessant fire without any good resulting from their undaunted efforts.

There was work enough and to spare to clear the streets and houses in front and on each side of the Kashmir Gate; and from the time the two columns joined forces till night set in a continuous fight was maintained. The system of attack in which we were engaged allowed of no formation being retained. Isolated groups of men, European and native, led sometimes by officers, and often without any leaders, roamed through the narrow streets, entering houses from which the fire was more than usually severe, and putting to death without mercy all who were found inside.

On one occasion a party of sepoys and armed rabble emerged from a house in our front, and were seen by our men, who immediately opened fire. Soon they were followed by a troop of women yelling and screaming. Keeping these as a cover for their retreat, the rebels got clear away, the soldiers having desisted from firing the moment the women appeared. This was a ruse which, I heard from others, was often adopted by the mutineers, who seemed to know intuitively that their women and children were safe from the fire of our men.

The deeds of individual daring performed during September 14 were numberless, and I was witness of many feats of arms and cool courage by the rank and file and non-commissioned officers of the different regiments. A private of my corps, a huge Grenadier Irishman named Moylan, saved the life of an officer under circumstances which fully entitled him to the coveted distinction of the Victoria Cross. In one of the numerous encounters which took place this officer, leading on a few men, turned sharply round the corner of a street, and was met by a force of sepoys coming from the opposite direction. A shot struck him, and he was felled to the ground from the blow of a sword, and would have been quickly despatched had not Moylan rushed to his rescue. Discharging his musket, he shot one of the assailants, and charged with the bayonet. This was broken off; and then, with firelock clubbed, he stood over the prostrate officer, dealing such fearful blows with the weapon—felling his foes in every direction—that the sepoys took to their heels, and Moylan, picking up the wounded officer, brought him to a place of safety. He was made a sergeant on the spot by the Colonel, but all efforts to obtain the Cross for this gallant fellow were unavailing. In those days the distinction was but seldom given; probably so many names were submitted for the General's consideration that only a few could be approved, and the application for Moylan was passed by.

But though in the latter's case the Victoria Cross was not given, it was awarded to a surgeon (named Reade) of my regiment on that day. He was ever to be found in the thick of the fighting, ministering to the wounded and cheering on the men. While engaged in his professional duties, a number of sepoys poured a deadly fire from the far end of a street into the group of wounded of which he was the central figure. This was too much for the surgeon, who, drawing his sword, called on some men of the regiment close by, and led them in gallant style against the enemy, whom he dispersed with great loss, killing two sepoys with his own hand. Not only on this occasion, but on several others, the surgeon's bravery was most conspicuous, no one grudging him the distinction he had so gallantly won.

There is nothing so destructive of the morale and discipline of soldiers as street-fighting, nor can control be maintained except by men of extraordinary resolution. The veterans of the European regiments composing the Delhi army on the day of assault fully justified their reputation. Cool and determined, they kept in check the impulsive valour of the young soldiers, and assisted their officers on various occasions when it became almost impossible to control their ardour. Till late at night the fighting never ceased; the weary and famished soldiers, exhausted and worn out from fatigue and exposure, and without a moment's rest, carried out the work of clearing the streets and houses, exposed all the time to a fire of musketry, coming chiefly from unseen foes.

Many lost their lives in the houses, where, entangled in the labyrinth of roofs, courtyards, and passages, they were shot down by the inmates, and were found, in several instances days after, with their throats cut and otherwise mutilated. The hope of finding plunder in these places also led many to their doom, and accounted for the large list of missing soldiers whose names appeared in the day's casualties.

And now I must pass from our force to record the doings of No. 1 and 2 Columns, under General Nicholson. These, for a long distance, had carried all before them, taking possession of the ramparts and bastions as far as the Kabul Gate, and effectually clearing the streets leading to the heart of the city. Exposed to a pitiless fire of grape and musketry through their whole advance, their loss was very heavy, but, still pressing forward, barrier after barrier was taken, the guns on each bastion, after its capture, being at once turned on the city. Their goal was the Burn bastion and the Lahore Gate, and all that men could do with their diminished numbers was tried at those points without effect. The rebels were in enormous force at these positions; field-guns and howitzers poured grape and canister into the assaulting columns, and musketry rained on them from the adjoining houses. Time after time attacks were made, till the sadly harassed soldiers, completely worn out, were forced to retire to the Kabul Gate and the bastions and ramparts they had already gained.

It was in one of these unsuccessful attempts to carry the Lahore Gate that Nicholson fell mortally wounded. Ever eager and impetuous, his dauntless soul led him into the thick of the combat. Spurning danger, and unmindful of his valuable life, he was in the front, in the act of encouraging and leading on his men, when the fatal shot laid low a spirit whose equal there was not to be found in India. He lingered for some days in great torment, expiring on September 23, mourned by everyone in the force, from the General in command to the private soldier, all of whom knew his worth, and felt that in the then momentous crisis his absence from amongst us could ill be borne. No eulogy can add to his renown; through his efforts, more than those of any other, Delhi fell, and he left his unconquered spirit as a heritage for the work still to be accomplished in the pacification of India. His name itself was a tower of strength in the army. Peerless amongst the brave men of his time, to what brilliant destinies might he not have succeeded had his young life (he was but thirty-four years old) been prolonged!

I must now revert to No. 4 Column, under Major Reid, and the attack on the strong fortified suburb of Kishenganj. About 100 men of my regiment were engaged in this affair;

and from the lips of our officers I had a full account of the fight and the subsequent retreat.[3]

The morning had dawned, and Major Reid waited to hear the signal to commence operations—the blowing in of the Kashmir Gate. His force, numbering about 1,000 men besides the Kashmir troops, were formed up on the Grand Trunk Road, opposite the Sabzi Mandi picket and at the foot of the ridge. Now the sun had risen, and still he watched for the signal, when shots in quick succession were heard on the right of the column, and it became known that the Kashmir contingent, without waiting for orders, had become engaged with the enemy.

Some men of the 60th Rifles were thrown out as skirmishers, and Major Reid moved with his force in the direction of Kishenganj. Soon they were stopped by strong breastworks thrown up by the enemy and barring the road to the suburb, the rebels being concealed behind these in great force, and pouring a heavy fire on our troops when only fifty yards distant. A rush was made for the earthworks, which were taken in gallant style; but the want of field-guns was here felt, and the enemy retired a short distance amongst the gardens, from which they continued to harass our troops. The Kishenganj battery also opened fire, and our position became critical in the extreme from the increasing number of the foe, who were constantly reinforced, and defied all endeavours to drive them from their cover.

While the struggle was thus raging on the left, the Kashmir troops on the extreme right flank had become involved with a large force of the enemy of all arms, who, no doubt despising the martial qualities of these half-disciplined levies, attacked them on all sides with great vigour. Our allies made no stand, and soon became completely disorganized,

---

3: Captain Deacon and Lieutenants Moore and Young were wounded in this engagement.

flying at length in headlong rout, with the loss of all their guns. No record was kept of their casualties, but they must have been very severe. For the future they remained unemployed in their camp, bewailing the loss of their four guns, and were never again engaged with the enemy.

Two or three days after the capture of Delhi I was wandering, with some others, through the streets of the city, when we came upon an officer and four men of the contingent, who accosted us, asking if we had heard or seen anything of their lost guns. They seemed in great grief, fearing the wrath of the Maharajah of Kashmir when they should arrive home, leaving the guns behind. With difficulty restraining a laugh, we assured them that we could give no information on the subject, and counselled them to search among the guns on the bastions near the Lahore and Ajmir Gates. They succeeded eventually in finding two, the others probably being borne off as trophies by the sepoys during the evacuation of Delhi. The contingent soon afterwards left for Kashmir, but how they were received by the Maharajah we never heard, though probably condign punishment was meted out to those who had actual charge of the guns.

The defeat of the Kashmir troops had a most disastrous effect on the issue of the attack on Kishenganj. Reinforced in great numbers, as I have related, the enemy maintained their ground, and our men could make no impression on them, chiefly from the want of field-guns. Major Reid, moreover, was wounded at an early stage of the action, and was carried off the field. His absence was soon felt in the altered dispositions of the force, and the want of a leader to carry out the plans formed by him.

The breastworks which had been taken could not be held for want of support, and some confusion resulted, the enemy's artillery from Kishenganj and musketry from the gardens causing great destruction. Many gallant attempts were made to drive off the rebels, but all were unavailing; and at length, after losing one-third of its number, the column fell back in good order to its original starting-point near the Sabzi Mandi, and Kishenganj remained in the hands of the enemy. Had that position been taken, and No. 4 Column, according to instructions, pushed on to the Lahore Gate, no good, as it turned out, would have been effected. Nicholson's columns, as related, had been forced to retire; the gate would have remained closed, and possibly the undertaking would have resulted in a more serious collapse than the ineffectual attempt on Kishenganj.

The presence of a large unconquered force on our right flank also placed the camp in imminent danger. It was known—from information received from spies—that it was the enemy's intention, after our failure to dislodge them from the suburb, to make an attack on the almost unprotected camp. The danger fortunately passed off, the rebels probably having little heart to join in operations to our rear when they heard the news of the signal success of our columns in the city. Still, their presence at Kishenganj was a standing menace; nor were we completely at ease with regard to the safety of the camp till the 20th, when the city was found to be evacuated by the enemy, and our troops immediately took possession.

Lastly, I must narrate the doings of the Cavalry Brigade. This force, with Horse Artillery, was stationed near No. 1 Advanced Battery, under the command of Brigadier Hope-Grant, their duty being to guard our right flank from being turned during the assault on the city. Here they remained, keeping a watchful lookout for some hours, till orders came for the brigade to move towards the walls of Delhi. They halted opposite the Kabul Gate, at a distance of 400 yards, and were at once exposed to the fire from the bastions, and to musketry from the gardens outside the suburbs of Taliwarra and Kishenganj. Our Horse Artillery made good practice, driving the enemy from their cover and spiking two guns; but the exposed situation caused great losses in the cavalry, and they moved still further to their front, halting amidst some trees.

The enemy now sallied from the gardens as though with the intention of driving the cavalry in the direction of the Kashmir Gate. The circumstances were most critical, when a body of Guide Infantry, coming up at the time, threw themselves on the rebels, maintaining their place with great resolution till help arrived, with a part of the Belooch battalion, and the enemy were forced to retire.

Too much praise cannot be given to the 9th Lancers and Horse Artillery for their conduct on this occasion. Exposed for hours to cannonade and musketry, unable to act from the nature of the ground, they never flinched from their post, forming a living target to the fire of the rebels. The same may be said of the Sikh and Punjabi cavalry, who displayed a coolness and intrepidity scarcely, if at all, less meritorious than that of their European comrades. Our casualties were very severe, the 9th Lancers alone losing upwards of twenty men killed and wounded.

And now that I have described the operations of each column and portions of the Delhi army during September 14, it will be necessary to record the advantages we had gained. From the Water bastion to the Kabul Gate, a distance of more than a mile, and constituting the northern face of the fortifications of Delhi, was in our possession, with all the intervening bastions, ramparts, and walls. Some progress had been made into the city opposite, and to the right and left of the Kashmir Gate, and along the line of walls. The College and its grounds, Colonel Skinner's house, that of Ahmed Ali Khan, and many other smaller buildings were held by the infantry. The enemy's guns on the bastions had been turned on to the city, and a constant fire was kept up, the streets and lanes being cleared in front, and advanced posts occupied by our men.

These advantages had not been gained without a severe struggle, and a terrible roll of killed and wounded was the consequence. Our casualties on September 14 amounted to upwards of 1,200 officers and men killed, wounded, and missing—a loss out of all proportion to the small number of men engaged, and when the relative forces are considered, far exceeding that which was suffered by the British army during the assault on the Redan on September 8, 1855. The deadly and destructive nature of street-fighting was here apparent, and the long-sustained contest, lasting more than twelve hours, swelled the total loss to the excessive amount recorded. In my regiment alone 100 men were placed *hors de combat*, thirty-three being killed; but the other European regiments suffered still more in proportion, and especially so those which took part in the actual assault on the breaches.

The native troops fought with the most determined bravery; Sikhs, Punjabis, and Goorkhas, side by side with their English comrades, pressed into the forefront of the strife, helping in the most material manner towards the day's success.

It was impossible to ascertain the loss sustained by the enemy. Dead bodies lay thick in the streets and open spaces, and numbers were killed in the houses; but the greater part of those who fell were no doubt carried off by the rebels. In the ardour of the fight many non-combatants also lost their lives, our men, mad and excited, making no distinction.

There is no more terrible spectacle than a city taken by storm. All the pent-up passions of men are here let loose without restraint. Roused to a pitch of fury from long-continued resistance, and eager to take vengeance on the murderers of women and children, the men in their pitiless rage showed no mercy. The dark days of Badajoz and San Sebastian were renewed on a small scale at Delhi; and during the assault, seeing the impetuous fury of our men,

I could not help recalling to my mind the harrowing details of the old Peninsular Wars here reproduced before my eyes.

With the exception of a small amount of looting, the men were too much occupied with fighting and vengeance to take note of the means of temptation which lay within their reach in the untold quantities of spirits in the stores of the city. Strong drink is now, and has in all ages been, the bane of the British soldier—a propensity he cannot resist in times of peace, and which is tenfold aggravated when excited by fighting, and when the wherewithal to indulge it lies spread before him, as was the case at Delhi. When and by whom begun I cannot say, but early in the morning of the 15th the stores had been broken into, and the men revelled in unlimited supplies of drink of every kind. It is a sad circumstance to chronicle, and the drunkenness which ensued might have resulted in serious consequences to the army had the enemy taken advantage of the sorry position we were in. Vain were the attempts made at first to put a stop to the dissipations, and not till orders went forth from the General to destroy all the liquor that could be found did the orgy cease, and the men return crestfallen and ashamed to a sense of their duties. The work of destruction was carried out chiefly by the Sikhs and Punjabis, and the wasted drink ran in streams through the conduits of the city.

September 15.—This untoward event considerably hampered the operations on September 15, and but small progress was made that day towards driving the rebels out of Delhi. The artillery and engineers worked hard at the completion of the batteries on the captured bastions, on which were mounted our own and the enemy's heavy guns; and one for mortars was erected in the College grounds, which shelled the Palace and the Fort of Selimgarh. A few houses were taken in advance of our positions, but no further movement on any large scale was attempted, owing to the demoralized state of a great portion of the European infantry, and, further, to a desire that the troops should obtain some rest after the unparalleled fatigues and exposure of the previous day.

Reports also spread through the force that the General, feeling his strength and means inadequate to hold even the portions of the city in our possession, meditated an evacuation of the place, and a retirement to the old camp to await reinforcements. Every consideration must be made for one placed in his critical position; and he, no doubt, in his own mind, felt justified in proposing the step, which, had it been carried out, would, in all probability, have ended in the fall of British rule in India. "In an extraordinary situation extraordinary resolution is needed," was the saying of the Great Napoleon, and to no crisis in our history was this dictum more applicable than that at Delhi in September, 1857. Mutiny and rebellion spread their hydra heads over the land, disaffection was rife in the Punjab, our only source of supply for operations in the field; and nought could stay the alarming symptoms save the complete capture and retention of the great stronghold of rebellion. It had also been a well-known maxim laid down and carried out by Clive, Wellesley, Lake, and all the great commanders who had made our name famous in Hindostan, never to retire before an Eastern foe, no matter how great the disparity of numbers; and history tells us that our successes were due mainly to this rule, while the few reverses we have suffered resulted from a timid policy carried out by men whose heart failed them in the hour of trial.

Happily for the Delhi army, and more especially for the English name, the counsels of the General in command were overruled by the chief officers in the force, and even the gallant Nicholson from his death-bed denounced, in language which those who heard it will never forget, the step contemplated by his superior officer.

Towards the evening of the 15th the enemy, becoming emboldened by our inactivity, attacked the advanced posts along our whole line, and kept up a sharp musketry fire, more especially on the College compound, while the heavy guns at Selimgarh and some at the magazine shelled those gardens and houses adjacent—even as far as the Kashmir Gate—occupied by our troops. At 5 p. m. a battery of heavy guns played on the defences of the magazine, soon crumbling the wall to pieces, and opening out a large breach for assault.

September 16.—My regiment, the 4th Punjab Rifles, and a wing of the Belooch battalion were detailed as a storming party, and mustering at an early hour on the morning of the 16th, we marched to the attack on the magazine.[4] This enclosure—a large walled area close to the Palace—was surrounded by a high curtained wall with towers, the interior space being occupied by buildings and containing a park of artillery and munitions of war. We met with no resistance on our way, and on approaching the breach saw only a few defenders on the ramparts, who opened a fire, which, however, caused little damage. A rush was at once made, the men gaining the top of the bridge without difficulty, and bayoneting some sepoys and firing on the remainder, who fled through the enclosure and were driven out at the gates on the opposite side. We had only about a dozen men killed and wounded, but of the enemy more than 100 lost their lives, being dragged out of the buildings where they had taken refuge and quickly put to death. Two hundred and thirty-two guns fell into our hands, besides piles of shot and shell; in fact, so vast was the amount that, although the enemy had been firing from their batteries for more than three months, making a lavish use of the stores at their command, scarcely any impression seemed to have been made on it.

4: Colonel Deacon, Her Majesty's 61st Regiment, commanded on this occasion.

That day and the following night our position in the captured magazine was anything but pleasant. The rebels continually harassed us with shells fired from the Chandni Chauk and near the Palace. Some, more venturesome than the rest, climbed on ladders to the top of the walls, plying us with musketry and hand-grenades, while others during the night mounted the high trees overhanging the enclosure, and with long lighted bamboos tried to set fire to the thatched buildings and blow up a small magazine. These attempts kept us constantly on the alert; and it was with great difficulty that we prevented damage being done.

Fighting continued during the day among the other portions of the force, and Nos. 1 and 2 Columns made further advances among the streets, the guns and mortars from the bastions throwing shot and shell far into the crowded parts of the city. Houses in commanding situations were taken and made secure from assault by defences of sandbags. Great judgment was shown in these operations, and the losses in consequence were comparatively few; but the enemy as yet gave no signs of retreating from Delhi, and our leaders felt that great exertions would still be necessary before the city fell entirely into our hands.

September 17.—During the 17th and 18th a constant fire of shells from upwards of twenty mortars was directed from the magazine and College grounds on the Selimgarh Fort and the Palace, those from the bastions still firing into a large portion of the city. Skirmishing went on at the advanced posts, and a regular unbroken line of communication was established from one end of our pickets to the other.

September 18.—On the 18th my regiment moved from the magazine and took up its quarters in the Protestant Church, close to the main guard and Kashmir Gate, and at no great distance from the northern walls of the city. This church had been built by the gallant and philanthropic

Colonel Alexander Skinner, C.B., an Eurasian and an Irregular cavalry commander of some eminence during the wars in the beginning of the century. He also erected at his own expense a Hindoo temple and a Mohammedan mosque, giving as his reason that all religions were alike, and that, in his opinion, each one was entitled to as much consideration as the other.

This church in which we were now quartered had been sadly desecrated by the rebels and fanatics of the city. They had, in their religious zeal, torn down the pulpit and reading-desk, defaced emblems, broken up the pews and the benches, and shattered all the panes of glass, while here and there inside the building were remains of their cooking-places, with broken fragments of utensils. The walls, too, had suffered much from the effects of our bombardment from September 11 to 14, the church being in the line of fire directed on the bastions. Many, no doubt, would consider it a sacrilege to quarter English troops in this sacred edifice, but the exigencies of war required its use for this purpose, and of all the buildings occupied by us during our stay in Delhi, the church was found to be cleanest and best ventilated, free from the noisome smells and close atmosphere of the native houses.

The close of the 18th saw our outposts extended hard by the Chandni Chauk—the main street of the city—the bank, Major Abbott's and Khan Mohammed's houses having first been seized by our men, who suffered severely from the field-guns and musketry of the rebels. There was also another unsuccessful attack made on the Burn bastion and Lahore Gate by the right column, in which the 75th lost one officer and many men killed. The arrangements for attack seemed to have been bad and ill-advised; the soldiers felt the want of the guiding genius of Nicholson, and, during an advance through a narrow lane were literally mown down by grape from the enemy's field-guns.

The weather, which since the 14th had been fine, broke up on the night of the 18th, and was succeeded by a terrific storm of rain, which fell in torrents like a deluge. That night it was reported that the rebels in great numbers were evacuating the city by the south side, the Bareilly and Neemuch brigades making off in the direction of Gwalior. Certain it is that from this period signs of waning strength appeared among the enemy, and fewer attempts at assault were made on our outposts, those on the left near the Palace, which were well protected by breastworks, being only exposed to a very desultory fire of musketry.

During the forenoon of the 18th there was, I think, a partial eclipse of the sun, which lasted three hours. The unusual darkness which prevailed astonished us beyond measure (our minds being taken up with events more startling than astronomical phenomena) till reference to an almanac explained the mystery. The eclipse had, we were told, an alarming effect on the mutineers, who attributed the phenomenon to some supernatural agency. The darkness no doubt worked on their superstitious fears, and hastened their flight from the city on which the wrath of the Almighty had descended.

September 19.—On the 19th operations in front of the Palace Gate were continued, a heavy fire being kept up against that place, while the 60th Rifles and others, perched on the tops of houses, took unerring aim at the rebels clustered in the open space. The same evening, also, the exertions of the right column were rewarded by the capture of the Burn bastion, with little loss on our side.

It was now quite evident that the baffled insurgents were retiring from Delhi in great numbers, mostly by the south side, few crossing the bridge of boats by day owing to it being commanded by our guns. But on the night of the 19th, when sitting in the church compound watching the shells exploding over the Palace and Selimgarh, we heard distinctly, through the intervals of firing, a distant, confused hum of voices, like the murmur of a great multitude. The sound came from the direction of the river, and was caused by multitudes of human beings, who, escaping by the bridge of boats to the opposite side, were deserting the city which was so soon to fall into our hands.

September 20.—After some sharp fighting, and early on the morning of September 20, the Lahore Gate and Garstin bastion, which during former assaults had cost us the lives of so many men, were taken, the column pushing on along the walls to the Ajmir Gate, which also fell into our hands. There were few defenders at these places, the mass of sepoys having evidently fled into the country; and the troops marched through the streets almost without opposition. There now remained but the Palace, Selimgarh, and the Jama Masjid, and these were all occupied by our troops on that day. The former seemed almost deserted, an occasional shot from the high walls directed on our defences in the Chandni Chauk being the only signs of animation in that quarter. Powder-bags were brought up and attached, to the great gate, which was quickly blown in; and the 60th Rifles, with some Goorkhas, rushed into the enclosure. A score or two of armed fanatics offered some resistance, but they were soon shot down or bayoneted, and a few wounded sepoys found in the buildings were put to death. Passing through the Palace, Selimgarh was entered, and this, the last fortified position belonging to the enemy, was taken possession of without a struggle.

Meanwhile, a force of cavalry under Hodson moved round outside the city walls, and found a large camp of the enemy near the Delhi Gate. This was deserted, save by some sick and wounded sepoys, who were put to the sword; and the horsemen, riding through the gate, made their way into the heart of the city and took possession of the Jama Masjid without striking a blow.

Delhi had at length fallen into our hands, and the toils and dangers of more than three months were at an end. The principal buildings were occupied by our troops, and guards were placed at each gate with orders to prevent the ingress or egress of any suspicious-looking characters, while parties of armed men patrolled the streets of the city from end to end.

That night we moved back to our old quarters at Ahmed Ali Khan's house, the 52nd taking our place at the church. The first-named building was a vast structure, belonging to a rich native, and had been furnished in a style of Oriental magnificence; but now nothing but the bare walls and floors were to be seen, the place having been ransacked of its treasures and completely gutted since our last occupancy.

From September 15 to 20, when Delhi fell, the force lost in killed and wounded about 200 officers and men, making the total casualties 1,400, including those of the day of assault.

From May 30 to September 13 inclusive 2,490 officers and men were killed and wounded, the grand total being close on 4,000. Add to these fully 1,200 who perished by cholera and other diseases, and it will be seen at what a fearful cost of life to the small force engaged the victory was won.

Truly the capture of Delhi was a feat of arms without a parallel in our Indian annals. The bravery of the men, their indomitable pluck and resolution, the siege carried on with dogged pertinacity and without a murmur, proclaimed to the world that British soldiers, in those stormy times when the fate of an Empire was at issue, had fully maintained the reputation of their ancestors and earned the gratitude of their country.

To me, after the long interval of years, the incidents of the siege, with its continual strife and ever-recurring dangers, come back to me as in a dream. Often in fancy has my mind wandered back to those days of turmoil and excitement, when men's hearts were agitated to their profoundest depths, and our cause appeared wellnigh hopeless. Then it was that a small body of men in a far-away part of North-West India, entirely separated from the rest of the world, a few thousands amongst millions of an alien race, rallied round their country's banners and despaired not, though mutiny and rebellion ranged through the land.

With steadfast purpose and with hearts that knew no fear, the Delhi army held its own for months against an overwhelming force of cruel and remorseless rebels. Imperfectly equipped, and with little knowledge of the dangers to be surmounted and the difficulties arising on every side, each man of that force felt himself a host, and devoted his energies—nay, his very life—to meet the crisis.

None but those who were there can for one moment realize through what suffering and hardship the troops passed during the three months the Siege of Delhi lasted.

Day after day, under a burning sun or through the deadly time of the rainy season, with pestilence in their midst, distressing accounts from all parts of the country, and no hope of relief save through their own unaided exertions, the soldiers of the army before Delhi fought with a courage and constancy which no difficulties could daunt and no trials, however severe, could overcome.

In the end these men, worn out by exposure and diminished in numbers, stormed a strong fortified city defended by a vastly superior force, and for six days carried on a constant fight in the streets, till the enemy were driven out of their stronghold and Delhi was won.

It must also be remembered that the feat was accomplished without the help of a single soldier from home; reinforcements had arrived in the country, but they were hundreds of miles distant when the news reached them of the capture of Delhi: and it is not too much to say that the success which followed the subsequent operations down-country was due mainly to the fact that all danger from the north-west had virtually ceased, and the mutiny had already received a crushing blow from the capture of the great city of rebellion.

CHAPTER 5

Occupation of the City

The renown won by our troops in 1857 is now wellnigh forgotten, and, in fact, their deeds in that distant quarter of our Empire faded into oblivion within a very short period subsequent to the capture of Delhi. When the regiments engaged at that place came home to England after a long course of service in India, scarcely any notice was taken of their arrival. There were no marchings past before Her Majesty at Windsor or elsewhere, no public distribution of medals and rewards, no banquets given to the leading officers of the force, and no record published of the arduous duties in which they had been engaged. Those times are changed, and the country has now rushed into the opposite extreme of fulsome adulation, making a laughing-stock of the army and covering with glory the conquerors in a ten days' war waged against the wretched fellaheen soldiers of Egypt.

Five years passed away after 1857 (and how many poor fellows had died in the meantime!) before a mean and niggardly Government distributed to the remnant of the Delhi army the first instalment of prize-money, and three years more elapsed before the second was paid.

In September, 1861, exactly four years after the storm of Delhi, my regiment paraded at the Plymouth citadel to receive medals for the campaign of 1857. The distribution took place in the quietest manner possible, none but the officers and men of the regiment being present. Borne on a large tray into the midst of a square, the medals were handed by a sergeant to each one entitled to the long-withheld decoration, the Adjutant meanwhile reading out the names of the recipients. There was no fuss or ceremony, but I recollect that those present could not help contrasting the scene with the grand parade and the presence of the Queen when some of the Crimean officers and men received the numerous decorations so lavishly bestowed for that campaign.[1]

The city was entirely in our possession by noon of September 20, and shortly after that hour I proceeded on horseback, with orders from the Colonel, to withdraw all the advanced pickets of my regiment to headquarters at Ahmed Ali Khan's house. These were stationed in different parts of the city, and it was with no small difficulty that I threaded my way through the streets and interminable narrow lanes, which were all blocked up with heaps of broken furniture and rubbish that had been thrown out of the houses by our troops, and formed in places an almost impassable barrier. Not a soul was to be seen; all was still as death, save now and then the sound of a musket-shot in the far-off quarters of the town.

My duty accomplished, I started in the afternoon with two of our officers to view a portion of the city. We made our way first in the direction of the Palace, passing down the Chandni Chauk (Silver Street) and entering the Great Gate of the former imperial residence of the Mogul Emperors. Here a guard of the 60th Rifles kept watch and ward with some of the jovial little Goorkhas of the Kumaon battalion.

1: Since the above was written, especial honour has been shown to those who participated in the hardships and glories of the campaign by His Majesty King Edward VII., who received the surviving officers at a levee at St. James's Palace on June 3, 1907. A public dinner was also given by the proprietors of the Daily Telegraph in the Albert Hall on December 23 of the same year to all the surviving veterans who had taken part in the suppression of the Mutiny in 1857.

From the first we learnt particulars of the easy capture of the Palace that morning, and were shown the bodies of the fanatics who had disputed the entrance and had been killed in the enclosure. None of them were sepoys, but belonged to that class of men called *ghazi*, or champions of the faith, men generally intoxicated with *bhang*, who are to be found in every Mohammedan army—fierce madmen, devotees to death in the cause of religion. Passing on, we wandered through the courts, wondering at the vast size of this castellated palace with its towering, embattled walls, till we came to the Dewan-i-Khas, and further on to the Dewan-i-Aum, or Hall of Audience. This last, a large building of white marble on the battlements overhanging the River Jumna, was now the headquarters of the General and his staff, and where formerly the descendants of the great warrior Tamerlane held their court, British officers had taken up their abode; and infidels desecrated those halls, where only "true believers" had assembled for hundreds of years.

Passing thence through a gateway and over a swinging bridge, we entered the old fort of Selimgarh, built, like the Palace, on the banks of the river, its battlements, as well as those of the latter place on its eastern side, being washed by the waters of the Jumna. Several heavy guns and mortars were mounted on the walls of the fort, and we noticed one old cannon of immense size for throwing stone balls, but which was cracked at the muzzle, and evidently had not been used for centuries. The fort was full of large and commodious buildings, used afterwards for hospitals by our troops, the place itself, from its commanding situation open and separate from the rest of the city, being the healthiest place that could be found. There was a lovely view of the country on the left bank of the Jumna, while to the north and south we followed the windings of the broad river till lost to view in the far distance.

Descending from Selimgarh, we took our stand on the

bridge of boats now deserted in its whole length, but over which, during the days of the siege, thousands of mutineers had marched to swell the rebel forces in Delhi. Thence we skirted along the banks of the river outside the walls, viewing on our way the houses of the European residents, built in charming situations close to the water's edge. These had been all entirely destroyed, gutted, and burnt; nothing but the bare walls were left standing, and the interiors filled with heaps of ashes. We thought of the wretched fate of the former inmates of these houses, most of whom had been mercilessly killed by the city rabble, urged on in their fiendish work by the native soldiers, of the regular army.

The mutineers of the 3rd Light Cavalry from Meerut had entered Delhi on May 11, crossing the Jumna by the bridge of boats, and, being joined by the city scoundrels, first wreaked their vengeance on the European residents who lived close by, and who, without any previous warning of the terrible fate in store for them, fell easy victims to the murderers. It made our blood run cold, when visiting the ruins of these houses, to think of the dastardly crimes which had been committed in and around the spots on which we were standing. Defenceless and unarmed, helpless in the hands of these human tigers, our unfortunate men, women, and children were immolated without mercy. Turning back, we entered the city by the Calcutta Gate, and walked along the ramparts by the riverside, past the walls of the magazine, till we reached the Water bastion. Here the destructive effect of our batteries during the bombardment was most apparent. Fired at the distance of only 180 yards, the guns had smashed the walls and ramparts to pieces, huge fragments had rolled down into the ditch, and the cannon in the battery were completely dismounted from the carriages, lying in confusion one on top of the other.

At the Kashmir Gate there was a heap of goods (consisting principally of clothes and rubbish) many feet high, which had been looted from the houses around. The guard at the gate had orders to allow no one to pass out with a bundle of any kind; and the consequence was an accumulation of material, chiefly worthless, which covered many square yards of ground. I have omitted all record of the plundering which up to this time, and for long afterwards, took place all over the city where our troops had penetrated. This account I have reserved for the last chapter, where full details of the loot of Delhi and the amount of prize-money accruing to the force will be found. September 21.—During the 21st I, in company with other officers, wandered over the heart of the city, continuing our perambulations south of the Chandni Chauk and penetrating into streets beyond, where the six days' fighting had taken place. The night before we had heard occasional shots fired at no great distance, and these were continued during the day and for some time afterwards.

Looting was going on to a great extent, both European and native soldiers engaging in the work; and though strict orders had been issued to prevent such licence, it was found impossible to check the evil. The shots emanated from these men, who, of course, went about well armed, and brooked no interference when in the act of securing booty. Altercations of a serious nature had taken place between the Europeans and Sikh soldiers, ending sometimes in blows, and often in bloodshed, when the two parties met in a house or were busy employed in dividing the spoil. However, in time, when most of the native troops had left Delhi, and the European regiments were quartered in walled enclosures with a guard at the gates to prevent egress, the looting on the part of the private soldiers ceased, and the prize agents were enabled to gather in the enormous wealth of the city without any trouble.

The portions of the town we passed through on that day had been pillaged to the fullest extent. Not content with ransacking the interior of each house, the soldiers had broken up every article of furniture, and with wanton destruction had thrown everything portable out of the windows. Each street was filled with a mass of debris consisting of household effects of every kind, all lying in inextricable confusion one on top of the other, forming barricades—from end to end of a street—many feet high. We entered several of the large houses belonging to the wealthier class of natives, and found every one in the same condition, turned inside out, their ornaments torn to pieces, costly articles, too heavy to remove, battered into fragments, and a general air of desolation pervading each building. Much of this wholesale destruction was, no doubt, attributable to the action of the sepoys and rabble of the city, who during the siege, and in the state of anarchy which prevailed during that period, had looted to their hearts' content, levying blackmail on the richer inhabitants and pursuing their evil course without let or hindrance. Still, that which had escaped the plundering and devastating hands of the sepoys was most effectually ruined by our men. Not a single house or building remained intact, and the damage done must have amounted to thousands of pounds.

We were quite alone in most streets; deserted and silent, they resembled a city of the dead on which some awful catastrophe had fallen. It was difficult to realize that we were passing through what had been, only a few days before, the abode of thousands of people. What had become of them, and by what magic influence had all disappeared? Not till days afterwards was the mystery solved.

The *tai-khanas*, or underground rooms of houses, scattered all over the city, were found to be filled with human beings—those who, by age or infirmity, had been unable to join in the general exodus which had taken place during the last days of the siege. Hundreds of old men, women and children, were found huddled together, half starved, in these places, the most wretched-looking objects I ever saw. There was no means of feeding them in the city, where their presence also would have raised a plague and many would have died; so, by the orders of the General, they were turned out of the gates of Delhi and escorted into the country. It was a melancholy sight, seeing them trooping out of the town, hundreds passing through the Lahore Gate every day for a whole week. We were told that provisions had been collected for their use at a place some miles distant, and it is to be hoped the poor creatures were saved from starvation; but we had our doubts on the subject, and, knowing how callous with regard to human suffering the authorities had become, I fear that many perished from want and exposure.

There were other objects also which raised feelings of pity in our minds. During our walks through the streets we caught sight of dozens of cats and tame monkeys on the roofs of the houses, looking at us with most woe-begone countenances, the latter chattering with fear. These, as well as birds of every description left behind in cages by their owners on their flight, literally starved to death in the houses and streets of the city. There was no food for such as these, and it is lamentable to think of the torture and suffering the poor pet creatures endured till death put an end to their misery.

Dead bodies of sepoys and city inhabitants lay scattered in every direction, poisoning the air for many days, and raising a stench which was unbearable. These in time were almost all cleared away by the native scavengers, but in some distant streets corpses lay rotting in the sun for weeks, and during my rides on duty, when stationed at the Ajmir Gate, I often came across a dead body which had escaped search.

On the afternoon of the 21st a most important capture was effected by Hodson. Shah Bahadoor Shah, the old King

135

of Delhi, was taken by that officer near the city while endeavouring to escape down-country.

Hodson, with his accustomed daring, and accompanied by 100 only of his own troopers, seized the person of the King from amongst thousands of armed dependents and rabble, who, awed by his stern demeanour, did not raise a hand in resisting the capture. The King was brought to Delhi the same day, and lodged as a prisoner in the house formerly the residence of the notorious Begum Sumroo. He was guarded by fifty men of my regiment, under command of a Lieutenant; and on the 22nd I went to see him, accompanied by our Adjutant.

Sitting cross-legged on a cushion placed on a common native charpoy, or bed, in the verandah of a courtyard, was the last representative of the Great Mogul dynasty. There was nothing imposing in his appearance, save a long white beard which reached to his girdle. About middle height, and upwards of seventy years old, he was dressed in white, with a conical-shaped turban of the same colour and material, while at his back two attendants stood, waving over his head large fans of peacocks' feathers, the emblem of sovereignty—a pitiable farce in the case of one who was already shorn of his regal attributes, a prisoner in the hands of his enemies. Not a word came from his lips; in silence he sat day and night, with his eyes cast on the ground, and as though utterly oblivious of the condition in which he was placed. On another bed, three feet from the King, sat the officer on guard, while two stalwart European sentries, with fixed bayonets, stood on either side. The orders given were that on any attempt at a rescue the officer was immediately to shoot the King with his own hand.

The old King was brought to trial shortly afterwards at the palace, and found guilty of complicity in the murders of our country men and women, and was transported beyond the seas, dying in British Burmah before he could be removed to the Andaman Islands, where, in accordance with his sentence, he was to have remained in imprisonment for the term of his natural life. The vicissitudes of fortune, numberless as are the instances among men of royal birth, can scarcely show anything more suggestive of the transitoriness of earthly pomp and grandeur than the case of the last King of Delhi. Sprung from the line of the great conqueror Tamerlane, the lineal descendant of the magnanimous Akbar and of Shah Jehan the magnificent, he ended his days as a common felon, far from the country of his ancestors, unwept for and unhonoured.

September 22.—Lieutenant Hodson, also on the 22nd, took prisoner, at a place some miles from Delhi, the two eldest sons and the grandson of the King. These men, more especially the eldest, who was Commander-in-Chief of the rebel army, had been deeply implicated in the murders of May 11, had urged on the sepoys and populace in their cruel deeds, and were present at the terrible massacre of our people which took place in the Chandni Chauk on that day.

Hodson's orders were precise as to the fate of these blood-thirsty ruffians, and though his name has been vilified and his reputation tarnished by so-called humanitarians for the course he adopted in ridding the world of the miscreants, he was upheld in the deed by the whole Delhi army, men in every respect better qualified to form a judgment in this particular than the sentimental beings at home who denounced with horror this perfectly justifiable act of speedy and condign punishment.

The three Princes were placed in a *gharee*, or native carriage, and, guarded by Hodson's native troopers, were conducted towards the city. Before they entered, the carriage was stopped, and Hodson spoke to his men of the crimes committed by the prisoners. Then, dismounting from his horse and opening the door of the gharee, he fired two shots from a Colt's revolver into each of their hearts. After being driven to the Kotwali, or chief magistrate's house, in the centre of the Chandni Chauk, on the very spot where our country men and women had suffered death, the three bodies were stripped save a rag around the loins, and laid naked on the stone slabs outside the building.

Here I saw them that same afternoon; nor can it be said that I or the others who viewed the lifeless remains felt any pity in our hearts for the wretches on whom had fallen a most righteous retribution for their crimes. The eldest was a strong, well-knit man in the prime of life, the next somewhat younger, while the third was quite a youth not more than twenty years of age. Each of the Princes had two small bullet-holes over the region of the heart, the flesh singed by gunpowder, as the shots were fired close; a cloth covered part of the loins, but they were otherwise quite naked. There was a guard, I think, of Coke's Rifles stationed at the Kotwali, and there the bodies remained exposed for three days, and were then buried in dishonoured graves.

On the 22nd the regiment, or what was left of it, comprising about 180 effective rank and file, moved from Ahmed Ali Khan's house to the Ajmir Gate at the extreme south-western side of the city, a distance of a mile and a half from our former residence. Here we put up in a large serai, with open courtyards in the centre, shaded by high trees, the small rooms on each side of the building being turned into quarters for the men, the officers taking up their abode in a mosque at the far end. The change was far from agreeable; flies and mosquitoes swarmed around us, the ditch outside the walls was filled with pools of stagnant water, and a horrible stench impregnated the air, increasing the sickness among the already enfeebled soldiers, and still further reducing our scanty number.

September 23.—The next day I started with D——, of my regiment, to view the Jama Masjid, or Great Mosque.

Nothing can exceed the rich, though chaste, beauty of this glorious structure. The building stands in a large walled enclosure, high broad steps leading up to the mosque, with its three domes of pure white marble and floor of the same material, all inlaid with figures. We ascended one of the minarets, about 120 feet high, obtaining a grand view of the imperial city and the surrounding country. To the south extended the ruins of Ferozebad, or ancient Delhi; to the east lay the River Jumna; and to the west and north stretched a forest of trees and gardens, among which were seen the suburbs of the city, the now historic ridge in the far distance hiding the whole camp from our view. From our elevated position a just estimate could be formed of the great size of Delhi: the city lay spread out below with its vast area of streets, its palaces, mosques, and temples, all silent and deserted, in striking contrast to the din and turmoil of a few days back.

Major Coke's corps of Punjab Rifles were quartered in the Masjid—a luxurious place of residence—but there were no worshippers to be found in the sacred building, and only armed men of an infidel creed were to be seen. A report spread at this time that it had been decided to blow up the mosque. I cannot vouch for the truth of this statement, and can only attribute the rumour to a belief that a large ransom would be paid by the Mohammedan population of India for the preservation of their temple had the authorities really intended to carry out the project. Its destruction would have been an act of vandalism quite at variance with the character of the British nation, and one which would have brought down on us the wrath and contempt of the whole civilized world.

From the Jama Masjid we wandered through narrow lanes and back-slums—the former resort of the worst characters in the city—to the Delhi and Turkoman Gates, the streets, as in other parts, being strewed with property from the wrecked houses, and wellnigh impassable. We saw parties of Europeans and native soldiers, all eager in the pursuit of plunder, going from house to house, or diving down courts and alleys when they saw us approaching. Interference or remonstrance with these men would have been useless, if not dangerous; in their excited state they were no respecters of persons, and we deemed it the better judgment to take no notice of their actions. Dead bodies lay in almost every street, rotting in the burning sun, and the effluvium was sickening, so that we were glad to make our way back to the Ajmir Gate to a less poisonous atmosphere.

A movable column of 2,500 men of all arms started on the morning of the 23rd in pursuit of the rebels, taking the direction to Cawnpore. My regiment had been detailed for this service; and, though numerically weak, and suffering from sickness, the officers and men hailed with pleasure the approaching departure from Delhi. But, unfortunately for us, the Colonel in command reported us sick and unfit to march. We were all to a man furious at this; everyone fit for duty was willing, heart and soul, to be sent wherever the exigencies of the war required, and more especially looked forward with delight to the prospect of serving under Sir Colin Campbell, in whose brigade the regiment had fought in the Punjab campaign of 1848-49. Still, the decision of the responsible officer was not to be disputed, and so the regiment was kept at Delhi.

On the 25th I mounted guard with fifty men at the Lahore Gate. The orders were "on no account to allow soldiers, either European or native, nor camp-followers without passes, to enter or leave the city." My post was constantly at the gate, where I examined passes; and while thus occupied some thirty troopers of the Mooltani Horse—wild, truculent-looking fellows, armed to the teeth—rode up demanding entrance. I explained to them what my orders were, and refused admission. Whereupon they commenced talking among themselves, and presently had the audacity to move towards the sentries with the intention of forcing their way. I was exasperated beyond measure, and turned out the guard, at the same time telling the Mooltanis that, if they did not at once retire, I would fire upon them without more ado. They then at once changed their threatening attitude, contented themselves with swearing at the *Gore log*,[2] and rode away, saying that now Nicholson was dead no one cared for them, and they would return to their homes. These men had been newly raised, were scarcely under proper discipline, and were certainly horrible-looking bandits and cut-throats—very different from the Sikh and Punjabi Horsemen, who were in manner and discipline all that could be desired. I knew that the Mooltanis only desired entrance into the city to participate in the looting which was still going on; and had they been allowed to indulge in a work for which by their evil countenances they seemed well adapted, collisions would have taken place between them and the English soldiers and others, and bloodshed would have been the result.

Shortly after the Mooltani Horsemen rode away I saw a party of Goorkhas coming towards the gate. They were strolling along quite unconcernedly, laughing and chatting together, with their hands in their pockets and quite unarmed, not even carrying their favourite *kukri*. Coming to where I was standing just outside the gate, they laughingly asked me to allow them to take a stroll down the Chandni Chauk and through a part of the city for a short time. My orders were imperative, and I told them so; whereat they said they belonged to the Sirmoor battalion—the gallant regiment which, in conjunction with the 60th Rifles, had defended the right of our position throughout the siege. The corps was still stationed at their old quarters at Hin-

---

2: White people.

doo Rao's house, and not one of them up to this time had entered Delhi. Naturally, they said they wished to see the city, promised most faithfully that they would refrain from looting, and return to the Lahore Gate in an hour's time. I found I could not resist the importunities of these brave little fellows, and, trusting to their honour, at last consented, though contrary to orders, to grant them admission. We watched them walking along the Chandni Chauk, staring in wonder at all they saw, till lost in the distance. Punctual to the time mentioned the Goorkhas returned, and, thanking me for my courtesy, made their way to their old quarters on the ridge.

During my tour on duty on this occasion at the Lahore Gate upwards of 500 of the Delhi populace were turned out of the city. They extended in a long string up the Chandni Chauk, decrepit old men and women with groups of young children. It was a pitiable sight, drawing forth exclamations of sympathy even from the rough soldiers on guard.

It had been brought to the notice of the General that some of the former inhabitants of Delhi, including sepoys, were in the habit of entering the city for the purpose of carrying away valuables, being drawn up by ropes held by confederates on the walls, and that many had also escaped in the darkness by the same means. Several captures had already been made, a strict watch was ordered to be kept at the several gates, and patrolling parties to march at intervals outside the walls. The day I was on guard at the Lahore Gate Hodson rode up to me from the outside, and said he had seen some natives on the walls close by, evidently attempting to escape into the country. I immediately sent round a corporal and four soldiers in the direction indicated, who presently returned with six natives—carrying bundles—whom they had made prisoners. All men thus captured were sent to the Governor of the city at the Kotwalli, who disposed of them as he thought fit, having the power of life and death in these matters. The Governor had the repute of being over-indulgent with regard to the disposal of the captives, being considered too merciful in his treatment of men who, for aught he knew, had forfeited their lives in joining the armed rebellion against our authority.

A striking instance of the feeling which animated officers and men in the troublous times took place some time afterwards at Delhi. An officer of my regiment was on guard at the Ajmir Gate, and on one occasion sent to the Governor some men whom he had captured while they were in the act of escaping from the city. These men were released; but on a second occasion three men were taken, and the officer, deeming it useless to forward them for punishment to the usual authority, called out a file of his soldiers, placed the prisoners in the ditch outside the Ajmir Gate, shot them, and then, digging a hole, buried them at the place of execution.

For a long period after the capture of Delhi executions by hanging were of common occurrence in the city, and the hands of the old provost-sergeant were full. Disguised sepoys and inhabitants taken with arms in their possession had short shrift, and were at once consigned to the gallows, a batch of ten one day suffering death opposite the Kotwali.

In the beginning of October two more reputed sons of the old King were shot by sentence of court-martial. They had commanded regiments of the rebel army, and were foremost in the revolt, even joining in the massacre of our people. The 60th Rifles and some Goorkhas formed the firing party, and took, strange to say, such bad aim that the provost-sergeant had to finish the work by shooting each culprit with a pistol. Nothing could have been more ill-favoured and dirty than the wretched victims; but they met their fate in silence and with the most dogged composure.

September 28.—Accompanied by our Adjutant and some other officers, I rode out to Taliwarra and Kishenganj

143

on September 28. These suburbs were a mass of ruins, but enough was left intact to show the immense strength of the enemy's position at the former place. Batteries had been erected at every available spot, strongly fortified and entrenched, and one in particular which had raked the right of our position was perfect in every detail, and was guarded by a ditch, or rather nallah, forty feet deep.

We passed through the large *caravanserai*, the scene of the conflict during the memorable sortie of July 9, and when in the course of our inspection in the enclosure a ludicrous event occurred. An officer who had been shot through the leg on that day, recognizing the place where he had received his wound, dismounted from his horse, and stood on the very spot. He was in the act of explaining events, and describing his sensations when shot, when suddenly he made a jump in the air, uttering a cry of pain, and commenced rubbing his legs, first one and then the other. We burst into laughter at the antics of our friend, who, we imagined, had been seized with a fit of madness quite at variance with his usual quiet demeanour, and jokingly asked him what was the matter. Still writhing with pain, and engaged in his involuntary saltatory exercise, he pointed to a swarm of wasps which, roused from their nest, on which he had been standing, covered his lower extremities, and had made their way inside his pantaloons, stinging him on both legs, and crawling up his body. The pain must have been intense, and fully accounted for his gymnastics and frantic efforts to crush the insects. It was some days before he recovered from the wounds he had received, far more painful—as he averred—than the enemy's bullet, I intimated at the time to my friend that the wasps probably were the ghosts of the sepoys who had been killed in the *serai*, their bodies, by the transmigration of souls, having taken the shape of these malignant insects in order to wreak vengeance on their destroyers. He, however, did not seem to relish my interpretation of this very singular event, and, in fact, was inclined to resent what he called my ill-timed jesting; but the story spread, and our poor friend became for some time afterwards the butt and laughing-stock of the regiment.

From Kishenganj we rode through the Sabzi Mandi Gardens, visiting our old pickets there and at the Crow's Nest, and then proceeded up the slope of the ridge to Hindoo Rao's house. This was still garrisoned by the Sirmoor battalion of Goorkhas, some of whom escorted us round the place, pointing out the different positions they had so gallantly defended. The house was knocked to pieces, the walls showing evidence of the enemy's fire, and revealing to us the truth of the saying in camp that these hardy little fellows, with the 60th Rifles, during more than three months, had been constantly exposed night and day to shot and shell, there not being a single part of their quarters where complete shelter could be found.

The Observatory, close to Hindoo Rao's house, had also felt the effect of the enemy's shot, while midway between the Observatory and the Flagstaff Tower, the Mosque—the only other building on the ridge—was also in ruins. Our batteries, nine in number, lay in a comparatively small compass, extending about three-quarters of a mile from the Crow's Nest in the right rear to Wilson's battery opposite the Observatory. The rest of the ridge was unprotected by guns in position, it being at so great a distance from the city and also free from the enemy's attacks; the only danger and annoyance arose from occasional shells, which reached the camp and exploded amongst the tents, from round-shot and from rocket fire.

Passing by the Flagstaff Tower, we rode through the old camp, now desolate and silent, visiting the graves of our poor fellows at the cemetery, and then, retracing our steps, entered Delhi by the Kashmir Gate, and returned to our quarters.

Cholera still continued its ravages among the small number of troops left in Delhi. The reaction from a life of strife and excitement to the dull existence we were now leading had its effects on the men, and we each day lamented more and more that we had not gone with the Movable Column, leaving the noisome smells, the increasing sickness, and the monotony of Delhi behind. Two thousand sick and wounded had been moved into the Fort of Selimgarh, where the pure air and open situation of the place soon made a marked change in the number of invalids: but disease was rife among the regiments quartered in the city, and convalescents from Selimgarh were soon replaced by men suffering from cholera and fever ague.

In the beginning of October, to our intense delight, we moved from the Ajmir Gate, that sink of corruption, and took up our quarters in the magazine. The officers here occupied a fine roomy building of two stories, while the men were housed in comfortable sheds round the enclosure. We still furnished guards at the Ajmir and Lahore Gates, the term of duty, through paucity of men for relief, extending over three days. The officer on guard at the former gate visited detachments and sentries at the "Delhi" and "Turkoman" Gates, a distance of a mile and a half through streets in which dead bodies in the last stage of decomposition were still lying. While one day engaged on this duty, I passed a carcass on which some pariah dogs were making a meal. Disgusted at the sight, and weak in stomach from the putrid air, I returned to my tent at the Ajmir Gate at the time when my servant arrived with my dinner from the magazine. I asked him what he had brought me, and was answered, "Liver and bacon." The nauseating sight I had just witnessed recurred to my memory, visions of diseased and putrid livers rose before my view, and, unable to control myself, I was seized with a fit of sickness which prostrated me for some time after.

Nothing of importance occurred during the month of October. We settled into a very quiet life at the magazine, varied by eternal guard-mounting at the different gates of the city and regimental drill. My health had been failing for some time, and, now that there seemed no immediate prospect of employment on active service, I gladly acquiesced in the doctor's advice that I should proceed to Umballah on sick leave.

November 8.—Accordingly I left Delhi on November 8, my destination being Umballah, a station in the Cis-Sutlej provinces. A *palki ghari*, or Indian carriage, drawn by two horses, awaited me that evening at Selimgarh, and, bidding *adieu* to our good doctor, who had nursed me with unremitting attention during my sickness, I entered the carriage. Just before starting, an officer of my regiment handed me two double-barrelled pistols—revolvers were at a premium in those days—saying they might possibly come in useful during my journey, and I little thought at the time that their services would be brought into requisition.

The country around Delhi swarmed with *goojars*, the generic name for professional thieves, who inhabited the numerous villages and levied blackmail on travellers, though seldom interfering with Europeans. My baggage, consisting of two *petarahs* (native leather trunks) containing uniform and clothing, was deposited on the roof of the vehicle under charge of my bearer, but the loot I had acquired, I had safely stowed in a despatch-box, which was placed under my pillow in the interior of the carriage. A bed, comfortably arranged, occupied the seats, and on this I lay down, closing the doors of the *ghari* when night came on.

Some two stages from Delhi, after changing horses and proceeding on the journey along the *pucka* road, I fell into a doze, and at last into a sound sleep. From this I was rudely awakened by shouts of "*Chor! chor!*" (Thief! thief!) from my bearer and the native coachman. Starting up, I seized the pistols, and opening the doors of the *ghari*, saw, as I fancied, some forms disappearing in the darkness at the side of the road. I fired two barrels in the direction and pursued for some distance, but finding that my shots had not taken effect, and fearful of losing my way—for the night was pitch-dark—I returned to the carriage. My bearer then told me that some robbers had climbed up the back of the *ghari*, taken the two *petarahs* between which he was lying, and made off into the country. We had been driving at the usual pace, about six miles an hour, and it proves the practised skill and agility of the *goojars*, who, with such ease, had abstracted the boxes from under the very nose of my servant. There was nothing for it but to continue my journey regretting the loss of my personal effects, but still fortunate in one respect—that the loot was safe under my pillow.

November 9.—At the next stage I questioned the horse-keeper, acquainting him with the robbery, and learned that a village inhabited by *goojars* lay off the road not far from the place where the robbery had been perpetrated. In the morning I arrived at the civil station of Karnal, and drove to the residence of the Commissioner, to whom I reported my loss, giving the name of the village where it had occurred. He told me to make out a valuation of the things stolen and to send it to him on the first opportunity. This I did on reaching Umballah, fixing the value of the different articles in the boxes at 250 rupees. A month afterwards, when the affair had almost faded from my memory, I received a letter from the Commissioner stating that he had visited the village near the spot where the robbery had taken place. The headman had been summoned to his presence, and warned that, unless the thieves were given up and the boxes returned with their contents intact, he would confiscate a certain number of cattle, and sell the same to indemnify me for the losses I had sustained. These orders being unfulfilled, the cattle were sold, and an order for 250 rupees was enclosed to me in the letter. The boxes, quite empty, with the exception of my journals, were found afterwards at the bottom of a well and were forwarded to Umballah. The ink had run in the journals from immersion in the water, but the writing was little defaced, and these papers—to me the most precious part of my luggage—I was glad to recover.

The change to Umballah was at first beneficial, but later on I suffered a relapse; and after appearing before a medical board, was granted a year's leave to England.

From Umballah I journeyed to Ferozepore, where I met several of my brother-officers and others who, like myself, had been invalided home.

January 10, 1858.—After a short stay there—the time being principally taken up with chartering boats and providing necessaries for the passage down the river—we all, to the number of about fifty persons, occupying twenty-two boats, which had to be specially fitted up with straw-built houses with sloping roofs, set off on January 10, 1858, under the protection of a guard of Sikhs, and, after what may on the whole be regarded as a pleasant trip, reached Tattah on February 11. Thence I went on to Karachi and Bombay and Marseilles, and, after a pleasant tour on the Continent of Europe, arrived in the Old Country in May, 1858, after an absence of rather more than six years.

CHAPTER 6
The Riches of Delhi

The riches of the city of Delhi and the opulence of its Princes and merchants had been celebrated in Hindostan from time immemorial. For ages it had been the capital of an empire extending from the snows of the Himalayas to Cape Comorin; and to Delhi, as to a centre, gravitated the wealth of the richest country in the world. Fabulous reports had reached us of the booty carried away to distant regions by the numerous warriors who burst like a torrent over Hindostan, making that city the goal of their conquests and the scene of their predatory forays. During the nineteenth century Delhi, since its capture by Lord Lake in 1803, had remained in the hands of the British, the city owing a nominal allegiance to the King, who, to all intents and purposes a State prisoner, was a pensioner of our Government up to 1857, holding a Court (consisting for the most part of wretched dependents and ragamuffins) in the Palace of the Great Mogul.

The quiet which reigned during that period had a salutary effect on the prosperity of Delhi; its merchants and storekeepers, trading with the inhabitants of the richly-cultivated Dooab and with more distant countries, became rich and prosperous, accumulating vast treasures, while the people, with the instinct of a penurious race, converted their ready-money into jewels and gold and silver ornaments, and safely stowed them away in hidden receptacles within their houses.

The numerous races of India—and notably the Sikhs—burning for an opportunity to plunder the imperial city, cast longing eyes towards these hidden treasures, the fame of which had spread far and wide; and to this desire may be attributed, as much as any other reason, the willingness of that warlike people to help us during the Mutiny.

While the siege was progressing, even at a time when clouded with anxiety as to the future, men's minds were full of the uncertain issue of the fight; the thoughts of all in camp turned involuntarily to the rich harvest awaiting the army should Delhi fall into our hands. To all of us (putting aside the morality of the question), the loot of the city was to be a fitting recompense for the toils and privations we had undergone; nor did the questionable character of the transaction weigh for one moment with us against the recognized military law—"that a city taken by assault belonged as prize to the conquerors." During the actual bombardment, when the end seemed at hand, this subject of prize was the topic of conversation among both officers and men; and soon we learnt with satisfaction that the General in command, after consulting with others in authority, had settled on the course to be pursued.

On September 7 a notice appeared in "orders" in which General Wilson thanked the army for the courage and devotion displayed during the long months of the siege. He recapitulated the dangers through which the force had passed, and looked forward hopefully to the future when, Providence favouring us, a few short days would see the enemy's stronghold pass into our hands. Instructions the most peremptory were laid down as to the absolute necessity for the troops keeping well together on the day of assault, and not dispersing in scattered bands or alone through the streets of the city in pursuit of plunder. Great danger and possible annihilation of the small army would result were these precautions overlooked, rendering the force liable to

be cut up in detail by the large bodies of rebels then occupying the streets and houses of Delhi. Lastly, as a reward
and incentive to all engaged, the General gave his word,
promising that all property captured in the city would be
placed in one common fund, to be distributed as prize according to the rules of war in such cases. The commanding
officer, as well as all in the army, knew that it would be
impossible to prevent looting altogether, but it was hoped
that the above order would have a good effect by urging on
the soldiers, for their welfare and advantage, the necessity of
obeying the instructions therein laid down.

This order, as I have said, appeared on September 7; nor,
from the promises given, had any of us the slightest doubt
but that its provisions with regard to prize-money would
be carried into effect in due course. Delhi was taken, but
as time passed by, and months elapsed without any noti-
fication on the subject being received from the Supreme
Government, the army began to feel anxious, and murmurs arose as to the non-fulfilment of the pledge given by
General Wilson. At length, at the end of the year, the Governor-General, with the advice of his Executive Council,
promulgated his decision that there was an objection to the
troops receiving the Delhi prize-money, and in lieu thereof
granted as a recompense for their arduous labours and pa-
tient endurance in the field the "magnificent" sum of six
months' *batta*.

Lord Canning, his Council and law advisers, all civilians
sitting quietly at Calcutta, living in ease and comfort far
from the dangers of war, thought, forsooth, that the Delhi
army, struggling for existence for months, fighting to up-
hold British rule in India—nay, for the very lives and safety
of these civilian judges—and at last victorious in the contest, would rest content with their decision.

It is needless to say that this roused a storm of indigna-
tion not only amongst the Delhi force, but throughout the

British army in India—a burst of resentment which, reaching the Governor-General, made him pause and reconsider his ill-timed and unjust decision. Suffice it to say that the order was rescinded, and that the prize-money, in addition to six months' *batta*, was granted to all engaged.

The day that the news of the first decision of the Government arrived at Delhi, when all at that place were full of the wrong done to the army, a private soldier of the 60th Rifles, inspired by the most exquisite sense of humour as well as of bitter satire, wrote upon the walls of the palace where his regiment was quartered the following appropriate sentence: "Delhi taken and India saved for 36 rupees 10 annas." It is said that the Governor-General demanded the name of this waggish soldier, with the intention that he might receive punishment for his daring effrontery; but it is needless to say that the author of the joke remained unknown save to a few of his comrades; and the great ruler of Hindostan was forced to rest content and ponder over the hidden sarcasm and bitter irony addressed to one in his exalted position.

The army was further promised by the Government 5 per cent, on the whole amount of the prize-money till the amount should be paid. This, during the many years which elapsed before the money was distributed, would have reached a large sum; but faith was broken and the sum repudiated—another instance of want of gratitude to soldiers who, looked to maintain their country's honour in time of war, are in peace, and when danger is at an end, soon forgotten. So prolonged, also, was the delay in payment of the prize-money that, I recollect, *The Times*, in reference to this subject about 1860 or 1861, had a leading article in its columns recommending the Delhi army to bring an action against the Government for the payment of the prize. Such action, of course, would have been without precedent, but it showed the feeling of many in the country when the leading journal thought right to draw attention to the subject with a view to the adjustment of the army's rightful claim.

To return to General Wilson's order of September 7. Notices were circulated throughout the camp in every brigade and regiment, calling on the troops to elect prize agents for gathering and receiving prize after the capture of the city. These prize agents, therefore, were selected by the army, one for the general and field officers, the second for the Queen's service of all ranks below that of Major, and the third for the company's army. The officers appointed, including Captain Fagan, and after his death Doctor Innes, Sir Edward Campbell, of the 60th Rifles, and Captain Wriford, of the 1st Bengal Fusiliers, were all most popular men, and considered in every way fit for the very important duties they had to perform.

On September 14, the day of assault, till the 20th, when Delhi was completely in our possession, much looting took place in the city. Our troops, both European and native, and especially the Sikhs, entered houses during those days and managed to secrete about their persons articles of value. To my certain knowledge, also, many soldiers of the English regiments got possession of jewellery and gold ornaments taken from the bodies of the slain sepoys and city inhabitants, and I was shown by men of my regiment strings of pearls and gold mohurs which had fallen into their hands.

On the day of assault we were much amused, during a slight cessation of the conflict, by one of our men rushing up to a group of officers in a state of great excitement, with the news that there was a buggy with two horses standing at the corner of a street close by. He offered the prize to anyone who would give him a bottle of rum; but in the then state of affairs no one felt inclined to burden himself with such a luxury, and the poor fellow went away much disappointed. Whether he succeeded in disposing of the prize I don't know; but when things quieted down, and the regiment was stationed in comfortable quarters, one of our officers, noted for his constant impecuniosity, appeared one day driving a buggy and two horses, the acquisition of which always remained a secret; nor would he, on being questioned, throw any light on the matter.

That many of the private soldiers of my regiment succeeded in acquiring a great quantity of valuable plunder was fully demonstrated soon after our arrival in England. An unusual number of non-commissioned officers and men bought their discharge, having during three years kept possession of the plunder acquired at Delhi awaiting a favourable opportunity for the sale of the articles. Many jewellers' shops in the town in which we were quartered exposed for sale in the windows ornaments and trinkets of unmistakable Eastern workmanship, which, on inquiry, we were told had been bought from the men.

It would have been contrary to human nature, and utterly at variance with the predatory instinct, had the soldiers failed to take advantage of the facilities for plunder which surrounded them on every side; nor could it be expected that a man, after possessing himself of valuables, would at once, or on the first favourable opportunity, deliver up his booty to the properly-constituted authorities. This much may be conceded, and it will therefore not be a subject of wonder that all ranks of the Delhi Force, with but few exceptions, availed themselves of the prize within their reach, and appropriated to their own use much treasure which ought to have gone towards swelling the general fund.

One officer in command of a native regiment quartered his corps in a house which formerly belonged to one of the richest Princes in the city of Delhi. The place was full of riches of every kind, and it was the popular belief at the time throughout the army that the officer in question succeeded in obtaining two *lakhs* of rupees. Rumour also said that a court of inquiry would be held to investigate the truth or otherwise of this report, but, if such had been contemplated, it fell to the ground; nor was any attempt made to induce the officer to disgorge his plunder. I paid a visit to this mansion some time afterwards, and can vouch for the thorough ransacking the place had received. Every room in the house had been pillaged, excavations had been made in the floors, and empty boxes lay in every direction.

Other cases similar to that just mentioned were known to us at the time, in which sums of money were appropriated only a little smaller in amount, while of those which reached the value of £100 their name is legion. Many men also there were who, at first swayed by moral scruples, as well as feeling reluctant to disobey the order which had been issued, refrained from looting on their own account; but when they saw that officers, even of the higher ranks, took possession of plunder, these scruples were cast to the winds—it was "every man for himself, and the d—l take the hindmost," and a general desire was evinced for each to enrich himself with the prize lying at his feet.

Often, when wandering through the city in pursuit of plunder, I, in company with others, came across officers engaged in the same quest as ourselves. These rencontres were most amusing, giving rise to mutual interrogations and many jokes, each party affirming that looting was not the object of their perambulations, but that they were only inspecting the houses out of a feeling of curiosity. Up to this time I had not succeeded in finding any articles of value, nor had I the remotest idea that my acquaintance with a certain officer in the employ of the prize agents would put me in the way of acquiring a fair amount of the loot of Delhi. A few silver ornaments and a small bag of sicca rupees were all that I had so far obtained, and I naturally felt desirous of increasing my store, more especially when it was well known that many officers, more fortunate and less scrupulous, had already made themselves masters of large quantities of valuable plunder.

The accumulation of prize by the agents began shortly after Delhi was taken. At first the articles obtained were of little worth, comprising chiefly wearing apparel of every description and household goods. Soon, however, more costly effects were found by the searchers, and in a very short time the rooms of the prize agents were filled with treasures of every kind—jewellery and precious stones, diamonds, rubies, emeralds and pearls without number, from those as large as hen's eggs to the small species used for necklaces; gold ornaments, chains of the most beautiful workmanship, bracelets and bangles all of solid metal. There were heaps, also, of the small, thick, native coin known as gold *mohurs*, thousands of which were accumulated by the prize agents and helped most materially to swell the amount. I visited one room, the long table in which literally groaned with the riches of "Ormuz and of Ind"—a dazzling sight to the eye, and one calculated to raise the spirit of greed in my breast to possess myself of some of the treasures so temptingly exposed to view. When quiet returned, and the inhabitants of the city began to flock back to their former homes, whole streets, in which no doubt treasure had been concealed and had escaped the search of the prize agents, were sold to the people for sums ranging from 5,000 to 50,000 rupees. All this helped to increase the prize to a sum which was variously estimated at from half to three-quarters of a million sterling; and even then it was asserted that only a portion of the vast wealth of Delhi had been found.

As far as I know, the Government, when distributing the prize-money in two installments—in 1862 and again in 1865—gave no account of the total amount which had been collected. The private soldier's share was reckoned as the unit, value about £17, increasing according to the pay of the different ranks—the Ensign five shares, Lieutenant six and a half, Captain eleven and a half, and so in proportion among the higher grade of officers, while that of the Commander-in-Chief amounted to one-sixteenth of the whole—an immense sum. There were, of course, many exaggerations as to how much each rank would receive as its share, and there were many heart-burnings also when the true amount became known. The sum had dwindled down to less than one-third of what we expected, and not a few expressed openly their conviction that some tampering had taken place with regard to the distribution. This can hardly be believed, though it has always been a notorious fact that the Government are inclined to treat the claims of those who fight their battles with neglect, and in one particular at least, by repudiating the 5 per cent, promised till the Delhi prize-money was paid, they acted up to their usual unjust policy, and gave occasions for the complaints which were raised at the time.

I will now proceed to give an account of my experience when acting as an assistant to an officer who was accredited by the prize agents with a permit to search for plunder. This officer, an old friend of mine, asked me to accompany him on his expeditions, saying also that he had no objection to my helping myself in moderation to part of the loot which we might happen to find. Carrying with us the necessary tools, such as hammers, spades, and pickaxes, we each day started—accompanied by two coolies—on our plundering excursions. For some days we were very unsuccessful, and for nearly a week only managed to gather together and transmit to the agents articles of little value. But, soon gaining experience from continued practice, and taking note of the different houses in which there was a likelihood of finding prize, we settled down to a systematic course of search, which in the end proved highly remunerative. Scarcely anything of value was found lying about the different rooms; these had been already gutted and the contents destroyed by the soldiers, both European and native, who, since the day of assault, had roamed about the city. At the time we began our search all was comparatively quiet, and during our operations, such was the vast extent of the city and so numerous the buildings, that only on two or three occasions were we interrupted by parties engaged in the same quest as ourselves.

My companion was a good Hindustani scholar, and taking advantage of his proficiency in the language, he made a point of interviewing several natives of the city, who, in the capacity of workmen in different trades, were allowed in Delhi, and were employed in their several occupations. From one of these, a mason and builder, N—received information that a large quantity of treasure was concealed in the house of a former rich resident. This man had helped to secrete the hoard, and on the promise of a small reward was willing to help us in unearthing the booty.

One morning in the beginning of October, attended by the mason, and carrying the necessary implements, we were taken to the house in question. This was a large building with a courtyard in the centre, the rooms of which showed the remains of luxury and wealth, but, as usual, had been despoiled by the plunderers of our army. Every article was scattered about in dire confusion; there were piles of clothing and bedding; rich and ornamental stuffs were torn to pieces, and the household furniture, broken up, was strewn about the courtyard. Our guide took us to a small room, about 80 feet square—in fact, it was the closet of the establishment—the walls of which were whitewashed, the floor being covered with a hard cement. Here, we were told, the treasure was concealed under the flooring of the room, and we lost no time in commencing operations, the mason assisting us. Picking through the cement, we came on a large flagstone, which we lifted out of the cavity. Then we dug a hole about 3 feet square, and the same depth in the loose earth, disclosing the mouth of a large earthenware *gharra*, or jar. Loosening the soil all around, we attempted to raise the jar out of the ground, but all our efforts were unavailing—its great weight preventing us from lifting it one inch out of the bed. Then, trembling with excitement, for we felt sure that a rich display would greet our eyes, we began slowly to remove each article from the gharra, and place it on the floor of the room. A heavy bag lying at the mouth of the jar was first taken out, and on opening it, and afterwards counting its contents, we found that it contained 700 native gold mohurs, worth nearly £1,200. Then came dozens of gold bangles, or anklets, of pure metal, such as those worn by dancing-girls. We were fairly bewildered at the sight, our hands trembling and our eyes ablaze with excitement, for such an amount of pure gold as that already discovered we had never seen before. But the treasure was not yet half exhausted. The jar seemed a perfect mine of wealth—gold chains, plain and of filigree workmanship, each worth from £10 to £30; ornaments of the same metal of every sort of design, and executed in a style for which the Delhi jewellers are celebrated all over India. Then came small silver caskets filled with pearls, together to the number of more than 200, each worth from £3 to £4, pierced for stringing. Others, containing small diamonds, rubies, and emeralds, and the greatest prize of all—reclining in a casket by itself—a large diamond, which was sold afterwards by the prize agents for £1,000. There were many other articles of value besides those I have mentioned—gold rings and tiaras inlaid with precious stones, nose-rings of the kind worn by women through the nostrils, earrings, bracelets, and necklaces of small pearls without number.

All these various articles we spread out on the floor of the room, examining each again and again, and with avaricious thoughts intent, lamenting that we were not allowed to appropriate what would have been to us a fortune. Truly such a temptation to enrich themselves without fear of detection was never till this occasion set before two impecunious subalterns of the British Army. Here, spread out before us, lay loot to the value of thousands of pounds, all our own were we to follow the example of some who had already feathered their nests with much larger amounts, defying those in authority to take the plunder from them. However, such a course could not be entertained for one moment, and, moreover, were we to possess ourselves of all the contents of the jar, there was no secure place of concealment to be found, and unpleasant inquiries and prying eyes would soon have revealed to the world our abduction of the booty.

It is impossible to do more than guess at the value of the plunder acquired on this day. My friend received a reward for the find; as for myself, I will leave it to my readers whether it was possible for weak human nature to resist the temptation of carrying away some few mementos from this miscellaneous collection of treasure-trove. To tell the truth, I must confess that in after times my only regret was that I had foolishly let slip an opportunity of enriching myself which could never recur. We agreed—and in this we were borne out by the prize agent—that £7,000 was the lowest sum at which to compute the loot we had found.

It was my invariable custom to wear as a *kammerband* or girdle folds of muslin round my waist for the protection of the liver and spleen, and in this I placed the articles I carried away. My friend procured a small cart, in which he deposited the loot and drove to the house of one of the agents, while I, encumbered as I was, with difficulty mounted my horse and rode towards the magazine. I could not but feel nervous and abashed when thinking of the riches concealed about my person, at last working myself up to such a pitch of excitement that I imagined all I met were cognizant of my good fortune; and on entering the gates of the magazine, I fancied I heard one of our men say to his comrade, "Well! that fellow, at any rate, has plenty of loot about him."

Our next great find, though by no means so lucrative as the first, brought a large accession to the prize fund. It occurred to me, through calling to recollection the story of the treasures concealed in the Hindoo idol at Somnath which was broken open by Sultan Mahmoud in the eleventh century, that possibly the same kind of receptacle might disclose a like prize, though on a smaller scale, among the numerous temples scattered through the city of Delhi.

Acting on this idea, we one day entered a small Hindoo temple situated not far from the Chandni Chauk. The shrine was gaudily decorated; but after a prolonged search, we found nothing of any value. A hideous idol stood on a raised structure in the centre of the building, and was soon demolished in iconoclastic style with our hammers. The base of the idol was formed of *chunam* (a kind of cement), and into this we dug with our small pickaxes. Soon a ringing sound from a blow disclosed a large silver casket imbedded in the *chunam*, and this, after some little trouble, we extricated from its position. Forcing the casket open, our sight was regaled by a brilliant show of jewels and gold—diamonds, rubies, and emeralds—two of the latter species being uncut, but of great size, pearls larger than any we had yet seen, and gold ornaments of every description, chains, bracelets, bangles, and a few gold mohurs. We were quite alone in the temple, and after feasting our eyes on the treasures and selecting a few objects for our own benefit, N—— took the casket to the prize agent, telling him where we had found it, and recommending a search in such localities, which recommendation, no doubt, was carried into effect among other Hindoo temples in the city.

When first entering a house during our search, we at once made ourselves acquainted with the creed of its former inhabitants. In this there was no difficulty—Korans lying about the floor denoted that the occupants had been Mussulmans, while many indications, such as idols, a different arrangement of the furniture, and other signs with which we became conversant, proved the influence of the rival Hindoo race. There was a very cogent reason for this investigation on our part—the Mohammedans invariably, in secreting their valuables, placed them in the ground under the floors of their houses, the Hindoos, on the other hand, always hid them in receptacles in the walls of the buildings. Armed with this knowledge, we used to sound either the floors or the walls of each house according as the place belonged to one or the other creed; nor in one single instance, as far as I can remember, were we at fault in our diagnosis.

A favourite hiding-place for valuables was behind the staircase, the treasure being concealed in a sort of vault built around with bricks and cement. On one occasion, in the house of a money-changer, we demolished a secret place of this kind and discovered four large bags filled with some heavy metal. Feeling convinced we should find that the bags contained at the least rupees, we opened one, and to our infinite disgust saw that the contents consisted of copper pieces called pice, of which there were many thousands; the bags, however, were taken to the prize agents, but I need scarcely say our hands on that day at least were not soiled by appropriating a portion of the plunder.

On several occasions we succeeded in finding large stores of money, chiefly sicca or native rupees, while in the houses of Hindoos, in portions of the walls which sounded hollow under the blow of the hammer, we, after making a hole sufficiently large for the passage of a hand, constantly brought to light large stores of silver ornaments, consisting of chains, bracelets, etc., amounting in the aggregate to a barrowful. Few houses there were that did not furnish, after a diligent search either in the floors or walls, some articles of value;

but on only one occasion after the successful ventures in the two first cases was the amount of loot in any way comparable to that which we obtained on those days.

In a very secluded part of the city, in a large house, surrounded by wretched tenements inhabited by the lowest class, we opened a door, and to our amazement entered a room furnished in the European fashion. This also had not escaped the marauding and destructive hands of parties of plunderers; the furniture was smashed, and the contents of the room strewn about the floor. There were English chairs, curtains, ottomans covered with antimacassars, sofas and broken mirrors, and in the corner a small piano, ruined and destroyed. The house had evidently belonged to some rich native, but who had been the occupant of this boudoir? for such it was—a miniature drawing-room filled with European luxuries, not excepting books and copies of music. Articles of a lady's apparel also lay about, torn in shreds, vases were on the mantelpiece, as well as a small box filled with English fancy needlework. We came to the conclusion that the mistress of this abode must have been a Eurasian lady, probably one of the zenana of the master of the house, who during the exodus from the city had fled with, or been forcibly carried away by, her protector.

A dismal mishap occurred to me in this room. Choosing a comfortable-looking ottoman, I sat down, little dreaming that I had fallen into a trap which would occasion much laughter among my friends for days to come. Feeling a strange moist sensation in a certain portion of my body, I jumped up from the seat, to find, to my horror, that I had plumped down on a quantity of *ghee*, or clarified butter. A jar of *ghee* was lying on the floor, and a portion of this horrible mess had been spilt on the seat of the ottoman. I was dressed in white trousers and jacket of the same material, and found, to my intense disgust, that the *ghee* had left a large patch of colour which no amount of rubbing would eradicate. We were far from our quarters, it was broad daylight, and, to my mortification, I was compelled to walk thus branded through the streets of the city, the laughing-stock of those who saw the plight I was in.

Delhi was celebrated for miniature paintings done on talc, hundreds of which were found at this time. Some were of rare workmanship, portraits of beautiful women and drawings of celebrated buildings, all executed in a style of art peculiar to the craftsmen of that place. We were fortunate, during our search, in coming across the house of one of these artists and disinterring from its concealment a box full of these paintings. They afterwards sold at a good price, and I possessed myself of some twenty of the most beautiful, comprising portraits of Zeenat Mahal, the favourite wife of the King, other ladies of the zenana, and pictures of the Taj and Jama Masjid, besides other mosques throughout India. These oval-shaped miniatures mounted in gold formed most acceptable souvenirs of the city of Delhi, and one in particular, containing the portrait of a lovely Eastern face with head-dress and tiara of diamonds, and strings of pearls round the neck, I was offered £20 for after it had been set in gold by a jeweller at Plymouth. In London, in 1858, there was a great demand for gold ornaments and jewellery from Delhi, so much so that a noted goldsmith offered me the highest price for articles of that description; nor would he at first—till convinced—accept my assurance that I had parted with all my Delhi loot before leaving India.

We were occupied for nearly three weeks in our quest for plunder, engaged in the exciting work almost every day, and seldom failing to find some articles of value. Our last adventure in that line deserves a detailed description, for though the nature of the loot obtained was such that it was useless to appropriate for our own use any of the goods found, still, the value of the plunder increased to a large extent the Delhi prize-money.

We had noticed in the room of the agents piles of *kincob*, or cloth of gold, worth I fear to say how many rupees a yard. The manufacture of this material was carried on to a great extent in Delhi, there being much demand for the rich and costly fabric among the Princes and nobles of Hindostan. Hitherto in our ramblings through the houses we had only come across a few pieces of this gold brocade; but as luck would have it, on the last day in which I joined N—— in his duties he had received information from a native that a large store of kincob was concealed in the house of a merchant who had dealt in that material.

The man guided us to the house in question; but after searching in every imaginable place, no signs of the gold cloth could be found. From the name of the merchant and certain other well-known indications we felt convinced that his goods were concealed underground, and we commenced tapping the floor of the largest room with our hammers. Presently, in the very centre of the apartment, there came a hollow sound, and digging down about a foot, we found a trap-door. This was lifted, disclosing a wooden staircase leading down to what seemed to us an apartment concealed in Cimmerian darkness. Lighting the wax candles we always carried about with us, we for some distance descended the steps which seemed to lead into the bowels of the earth.

The room turned out to be about twenty feet square and ten feet high, and ranged around, piled one on top of the other, were scores of large boxes. One of these we opened, and found it to contain *kincob* of the rarest kind; others that we looked into were full of the same gorgeous material, and we came to the conclusion that here, spread about, there was a treasure the value of which amounted to a *lakh* of rupees. Four large carts were loaded with the boxes and taken to the prize agents, the contents selling afterwards for a very large sum.

And thus ended in a most successful find my connection with the loot of Delhi. Though many years have elapsed, the events of those three weeks seem as vivid in my memory as though they had happened yesterday—the brightness of the jewels, the dazzling gold, the nerves wrought to the highest pitch of tension while waiting in eager expectation for the result of a search.

These episodes of my life appear more like a fairytale or a legend of the "Arabian Nights" than true history and sober reality. What opportunities of accumulating a small fortune were thrown in my way! The treasure lay at my feet, only wanting to be picked up, and many will say that I was a fool not to take advantage of the prize! I can, however, certainly aver that I showed great moderation in possessing myself of only a small portion of the plunder—the amount I appropriated was but an infinitesimal part of the Delhi prize money.

It is very unlikely that Delhi or any other rich city in India will be given over to sack and pillage, during this generation, but the remembrance of the days of 1857, and of the traditional wealth of the country, still exists amongst the nations of the East, and only recently, during the scare arising out of the Russian occupation of Merv, it was stated that the Turkomans, now feudatories of that Empire, cast longing eyes on Hindostan, "where gold and diamonds could be picked up in the streets of the large cities."

During my stay at Umballah I made arrangements with an officer of the Civil Service for the sale of the loot I had brought from Delhi. He entrusted the commission to one of his native writers, who executed the work in a satisfactory manner, though the price I received was hardly equal to the amount I had anticipated. To my friend's wife I gave a filigree gold chain of beautiful workmanship, and of such length that it reached six times round the neck, also a tiara of precious stones, while I also presented some pearls and gold *mohurs*. There is no doubt that, had I brought the whole of my plunder home to England, the price obtained for it would have been far in excess of what I received at Umballah, but the risk of transportation was too great; I feared, also, the chance of robbery and the anxiety attached to carrying about with me so many articles of value.

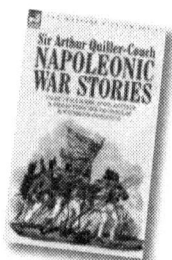

www.ingramcontent.com/pod-product-compliance
Lightning Source LLC
Chambersburg PA
CBHW021107090426